The Life of a Crime Scene Cleaner

By Ben Giles

About the Author

Ever since a small child I have loved solving problems, and I quickly realized that the more difficult the problem the more I could specialize, the faster I could respond – the more I could charge, the better I could solve the problem the more I would be in demand, this focused me to look for niche opportunities in life. I love living in rural West Wales with my amazing family and friends, I love the people, the countryside and living within a short walk from the coast. I have never been afraid of hard work, actually I love it! I get bored easily so constantly need a project to be enthused about. Me being an author feels out of my comfort zone! I feel like a builder in a suit! But like everything I do I have thrown my heart and soul into this and hope you appreciate all I have done and tried to achieve.

The Life of a Crime Scene Cleaner

It's a Wednesday afternoon. The sun is dipping beneath the cloud line on the horizon. I look across at Ash, sitting in the van next to me, and realise we have been silent since we left Brighton. We are approaching Bristol on our journey back to West Wales.

We don't really know the exact reason we are reluctant to speak, but we both know that the crime scene we have just cleaned up has affected us in a way we did not think possible.

On arrival at the property about six hours earlier, we were met by a WPC officer who told us that a middle-aged teacher had been bludgeoned to death by her husband. Apparently, they were both professional people, and had a beautiful house where they looked like they had the perfect life. Following the attack, she had survived on the kitchen floor for three days until her neighbour found her… but sadly died en route to the hospital in an ambulance.

A fine mist of crimson blood covers the entire room. Handprints and finger marks in blood litter the kitchen units. Dish-shaped lights have blood spray all over them. Almost every surface has blood on it; even drawers had blood inside them, underneath and inside the runners along the sides. The washing machine had so much blood on it that it had even run inside the door and into the seal.

A small pool of semi-dried blood sits centre stage on the vinyl flooring where the woman lay for three days.

As the WPC officer makes her way into the lounge to complete her paperwork, we begin to remove the liquid that once kept this woman alive from her kitchen. In a few short hours, we will remove every last trace of what has happened and be on our way back to our homes, our families, and our wives.

During my thirty years as a crime scene cleaner, I have personally cleaned up hundreds of properties where a violent death, murder, suicide, or decomposition has taken place. I have had to scrape decomposed body fat from the cracks in floorboards, scrape brain and body fluid from ceilings, and even dig down through a hoarder's collection of waste to uncover his decaying body for a Police SOCO to photograph. Then, when his body was removed, I worked my way through 4.2 tonnes of waste, smelling and dripping in his decomposed body fluid, bagging it and removing it to be incinerated.

This is my story, how I began, and how my business has grown into a national biohazard response and training company.

My Roots

My parents were, and still are, amazing people. They are true entrepreneurs. My dad worked as a caravan salesman and had a few other jobs before realising that he wanted to do something for himself. So, he started his own fruit and veg shop in Bedfordshire, buying local stock that supermarkets didn't want because it was oddly shaped, too big, or too small. He made a success of selling to his local community, employing many staff and having a delivery round that grew quickly and was recognised for its quality.

Wanting something more and driven by their passion to be self-sufficient, Mum and Dad trawled around the West Country and Wales in an old Landrover with three kids in the back, towing a caravan, looking for a smallholding to make their dreams come true. Smitten with the town of Cardigan on the west coast of Wales, they found a smallholding that looked amazing! With all the cash they had from selling their business and home, they bought 80 acres of Welsh countryside. They set about changing their stars—with me, three months old, my sister, one and a half, and my brother, a nipper at five years old—all beginning our new life in Wales!

This may sound run-of-the-mill now, or even like an Escape to the Country moment, but it was far from it back then. Very few people were making this kind of life-changing move at the time. Not many would take the risks associated with such a change, and I think that's where my ease with risk-taking was nurtured. Instead of having conventional parents who were happy working 9–5 for someone else, I had pioneers—risk-taking hippies! They were crazies who were willing to have a go.

They learned skills from locals, books, the local college, and informative day courses run by other pioneers. Within a few years, they had cows, sheep, pigs, and chickens. Mum even bred rabbits to sell for meat. Dad struck a deal with a local chicken farm next door for manure for the fields and managed to buy an old caravan, putting it in the paddock and letting it out for holidays. Having never built houses before, they managed to get planning permission on their land and started a development business. Fifteen years later, they had built and sold six properties, converted the barns into seven holiday cottages, built a spa with a pool, gym, and bistro, and opened a campsite—all of which were thriving.

The clever bit was this: they had a construction business, a tourism business, a property rental business, a spa business, and a farming business at the core of it all. When farming was financially bad, tourism boomed. When the housing market soared, they capitalised on it. Even when COVID hit, they had a property portfolio to keep generating income. My mentors were two people who not only loved me and encouraged me to take risks but showed me through their lives that the risk is worth it. They were not, and are not, the kind of people who look back and say, “We wish we had done this or that.” They did it in bucketloads.

I feel I should apologise to my teachers at school—especially secondary school. I really didn't see the point of most of the lessons and became quite vocal in asking questions like, "When will I ever need to know how trigonometry works?" "Who cares what a five-sided shape is called?" and "Will I ever in my future life need to know how an oxbow lake is formed?" I think my teachers were so indoctrinated by the school curriculum that they just followed rules written by someone who didn't know me, my local area, or what was actually needed to become self-employed. I do think they may respect me now for what I have accomplished, but I apologise for being arrogant, cheeky, and sometimes rude in how I questioned things.

I realised from an early age that I could change my life if I wanted to. All the influences from careers teachers and exam results really meant nothing to me. I looked closely at the people where I lived, examined their lives, and realised that in West Wales, a good name, a great idea, and a fantastic service meant more than any piece of paper stating you had completed an exam or a stretch of time at university. I struggled with the idea of working for someone else and saw many people moving from job to job because they didn't get on with their employer.

As such, I decided to start my own business. I hated being indoors, loved being outside, and became bored so quickly it was frightening! Hence, I knew I needed a job outdoors that changed from day to day. And no matter how daft it sounded, window cleaning fitted perfectly with my lifestyle. By the time I was 17, I was working three days a week, earning about £150 per day—and this was back in 1997! I managed to buy my first house at 18 for £13,000! Wow, how things have changed for young people trying to get on the property ladder!

Life was good. I had a great reputation in the community, which was really important to me, and I worked damn hard to build a successful business. I also sacrificed a lot. All my mates from school were lost to me almost overnight; they stayed on in school to do A levels and then to university. For me, it was just head down and making it work. I can't remember ever saying no to any work I was offered. Working from dawn to dusk became the norm, but I loved it.

One thing I also realised was that while local business people were complaining about road links and wanting routes to open up to bring more people to the area, I wanted the roads to remain small, winding, and hard to travel. This kept my competition far away! It gave me an advantage—living locally, delivering local services to local people.

Solve a problem - Start a business

It amazes me that there have been so many people who have built businesses based on ideas or problems that don't really exist, only to watch them fail—like the infamous cardboard sun lounger. Now, I'm all for recycling, but is there really a problem with wooden sun loungers? And would you want to get out of the pool soaking wet and sit on cardboard? Then there's the golf trolley that follows you around the course… I mean, really! Why invent something when there's no problem to solve?

Instead, I decided to look for real problems that needed solving—specifically in the cleaning industry. I've always loved identifying genuine issues and coming up with solutions. For instance, we were one of the first companies to make pole-system window cleaning systems. We used telescopic poles, polypropylene water tanks (my mate made those), and deionising vessels from a local water treatment company—all to address the problem of falls from ladders. This became a great income source for us for many years, with people travelling from all over the UK to have their vans kitted out with our systems.

As a team, we have designed lots of products and services to solve various problems—like scented silicone, scented bottle tops, scented wristbands, and even scented flooring (imagine the possibilities!). We've also developed sanitising cans that release enough sanitiser to clean an ambulance, and whisky sold in miniature barrels instead of bottles so it continues to age. But those stories are for another book!

I had a friend in South Wales who decided to buy a pallet of SKY TV dishes. He noticed they rusted over time and looked awful against beautiful, expensive houses. His solution? Offer to replace the rusty dishes with shiny new ones! Problem solved. And what did he do with the old ones? He took them home, sanded them down, cleaned them off, and gave them a fresh coat of paint—turning them into new stock. Genius!

A friend of a friend makes King of Shaves shaving gel. What was the issue he solved? When you cover your face in foam, you can't see your face! That one simple, problem-solving idea made him a millionaire.

There are still plenty of problems to solve—some massive, some small. For instance: How do we stop children in schools from sticking chewing gum under desks? How do we encourage elderly people to mix with younger generations to pass on knowledge and skills? How do we get children physically playing again instead of sitting in front of screens? These might be a bit deep for this book, but you get the point!

I love this kind of thinking. Instead of walking into a room or building and just sitting down, start looking for the problems, the issues, and the requirements needed to make a difference. I remember flying home from Venice with my wife, and we stopped at a service station. While she used the bathroom, I noticed that the glass atrium in the centre of the building was filthy! Before she had returned, I had found the manager and was quoting for the clean required! This culture of problem-solving now runs through my business. We focus on creating products and services that truly make a difference for people and businesses.

If you're thinking of starting a business, first look for the problems you can solve where you live. Even if you're competing in an existing market, ask yourself: Can you be quicker, more reactive, more efficient, kinder, or more careful? Anything that makes you solve the problem better for the customer is a winning strategy.

We've even identified problems we could solve, only to discover that another company was already solving them elsewhere. What did we do? We contacted them, congratulated them on their achievements, and offered to work for them on a subcontract basis in areas where they couldn't react quickly or had limited resources. This approach has led to us working with major companies as their last resort—if they can't self-deliver, they call ULTIMA, and we sort it out! Even the giant FM company Mitie calls us its USP!

I also realised that I needed to forget the word NO. If I had said no to every job I was asked to do that I'd never done before, there's no way I'd have become successful. Instead, I always said YES, and as a result, I became adept at many tasks I never thought I'd do.

As you read through these accounts and memoirs, remember this: It's only by saying yes to the first ever horrible job I did that all of this started.

By the age of 23, I had 20 people working for me. I ran a business recognised locally for services like window cleaning, carpet cleaning, office cleaning, gutter cleaning, pressure washing, high-level cleaning, kitchen deep cleaning, kitchen duct cleaning, post-builders' cleans, and student accommodation cleaning.

I was never deterred by the size of a task. I once received a call from a company due to hand over a new multiplex cinema in Cardiff the next day. Prince Charles was opening the building, but the cleaning company they'd hired had been caught stealing and kicked off-site.

"Could we supply 24 cleaners for 24 hours to clean the building?" they asked. "YES, we can!" I replied (excuse the Bob the Builder quote).

I phoned everyone I knew and managed to get 24 reliable people together. I hired a minibus and a van from a local taxi firm and headed to Cardiff. I hadn't even seen the building. All I knew was that it had 13 cinema screens, six floors, and was filthy! Oh, and the previous cleaning company had been booted off-site 36 hours earlier because one of their cleaners had stolen a plasma screen from the entrance hall the night before!

But we did it. I earned enough money to buy the van from the taxi firm called Robins, so I never gave it back.

The niche work was where I saw real opportunity. If I could solve the problems of truly terrible situations, I could build a great business. Tackling jobs people feared or avoided came with immense satisfaction. Knowing I had made things much better for someone was incredibly rewarding.

Now, I own a business that supplies professional biohazard cleaning across the UK, employing and subbing out to over 600 fantastic, trained operatives.

How did it start? What did I do? What have I seen? How did I feel?

I Have Never Been Afraid Of Getting My Hands Dirty!

Growing up on a farm meant that I was used to dirt, muck, and blood—even when I was a tiny lad of five years old. Mum loves telling people that, wanting to be like my dad, I went out hunting for rabbits with a wooden stick as a gun! Mum laughed as she watched me leave the house and begin walking across the fields until… I returned home with my stick gun in one hand and a rancid, stinking, rotten rabbit carcass that was the leftover catch of a fox, slung over my shoulder. With a massive grin on my face, I announced, "Look what I shot!" If my parents had reacted terribly to me, I think it would have driven the enterprise out of me! But Mum was so proud of me and exclaimed, "Well done—look what you shot!"

When you have a flock of sheep, lambing season is an incredible time! But for all young farmers, this time of year is both awe-inspiring and character-building. You see and have to do some messy, macabre things. At just six years old, I was helping to pull lambs from their mums. I also had to pull out a lamb that had died inside the womb and had already started to decompose. I vividly remember that event—and the smell!

When a lamb is born dead, we often had to skin the lamb and place its hide on an orphan lamb so that the mother of the dead lamb would adopt the skinned orphan. How many inner-city kids would even witness something like that, let alone experience it? I was regularly cleaning out poo from some animal—be it ducks, chickens, cattle, or pigs. This was just normal—what any farming family deals with—but it must have desensitised me compared to other kids whose parents would scream if they got mud on their new trainers! It was far different for me, a child who was most of the time filthy, covered in some sort of animal poo, and smelling like a used wheelie bin. But I was happier than a pig in muck—excuse the pun!

I used to have a farm set to play with—plastic animals, die-cast machinery—and my dad even built me a scale model Dutch barn to store it all in. I suppose it became evident that I wasn't afraid of poo or bad smells when I found a cat poo one of our cats had done and pushed it into my toy muck spreader, driving it around the room (my farm field), proud as punch, spreading what I thought was real manure on the carpet. Mum didn't go mental with me but again saw the enterprise, initiative, and creativity behind the mess!

As Mum and Dad embarked on their self-sufficiency lifestyle, they decided to have a local slaughterman come to the farm to kill one of their beef cattle. I was there when the bolt gun was used to kill it, and Dad used a pulley system he had set up in the barn joist to hoist the bull up by its back legs so it could be bled and butchered. I remember watching Mum kill chickens and rabbits, butcher them, and cook them for the family. Mum would even cut off the chickens' feet, leaving the tendons hanging out, and then let us play with them. We'd pull the tendons to make the feet move in and out, using them to pick things up. Chuff! Maybe my childhood was a bit weird!

A surreal moment for me was visiting my nan for the last time before she passed away. My nanny was English, and my Nonno was Italian. They had an amazing life with incredible stories and were true entrepreneurs. For as long as I had known them, they were antique dealers. Their original shop (under different management), Mannucci's Antiques, is still going in Bedfordshire.

When they retired, they filled their house with an array of trinkets and furniture, which I loved hearing about. They both loved enterprise, and I always felt they were so proud of how hard Mum and Dad worked—and how hard my brother, sister, and I worked in turn. Any time I was featured on TV or in the press for a job we had completed, they couldn't wait to tell me how proud they were. I miss them dearly.

On this last visit, Nan was in bed, and I sat by her side, talking to her. As usual, she told me how proud she was and asked how work was going. I told her we were busy. Then came the bombshell. Nan said, "I used to do that."

"What—cleaning?" I asked.

"No," she said. "Cleaning up after dead people!"

I was stunned. "WHAT! I've known you for nearly 30 years, and I never knew that!"

"Yes," she said. "I used to get first pick of the antiques if I agreed to clean up body fluid first."

Subconsciously, was this the reason I went into this line of work? Or the reason I could do it with ease? I'll never know. But I love the fact that another family member before me was also a specialist cleaner.

Age Concern

For many years, I carried on window cleaning, and it was a great job—when it wasn't raining, freezing cold, or when I was unwell and couldn't work. I realised I needed to diversify, to add some more strings to my bow!

My brother had moved to Hong Kong to do charity work, and I decided to follow him to see if it was something for me. I supplemented my charity work with teaching English (having attended Swansea University and completed a TEFL teaching course). I loved the work but hated the city—all those people crammed into one tiny place! The heat and humidity were also hard to deal with. Feeling proud, I completed a year outside my comfort zone, then returned to Wales and to window cleaning.

Before I left for Hong Kong, I met up with my childhood sweetheart. We had been friends for many years since her parents had a caravan on my parents' campsite. When I returned, we grew close again and decided to marry. That was 26 years ago now, and I love Linz more every day I spend with her. She's my best mate and my support in life—a truly amazing person who has been my rock.

I picked up my window cleaning round again upon my return to Cardigan and started over, but I looked for any opportunity to make money. I began importing Japanese sports cars from Dublin and selling them. I also started selling janitorial equipment and consumables.

My big break came when I was cleaning the windows for

the lady who ran the charity AGE CONCERN in Aberystwyth, Mid Wales. I remember talking to her in her garden in a coastal village called Borth. I told her, "I'm available to clean anything if you need help with anything beyond windows."

She replied, "Well, there's a property the charity looks after—a series of apartments. One of the tenants hasn't cleaned his flat in 10 years. The warden can't even enter because of the smell, and the two neighbouring flats are empty because of it!"

I immediately said, "I can sort the problem for you! Just arrange for the gentleman to be out of the house for a day, and we'll handle it."

Looking back, the naivety of what we were about to face is frightening! When we arrived at the flat, as soon as the door opened, the floor was moving with fleas. I shut the door immediately.

"How do you kill fleas?" I thought. Back then, there was no Google to check! So, I grabbed the Yellow Pages and found a pest control company. Pretending to be a pest controller, I said, "I've run out of gear to kill fleas!"

They believed me and met me at a petrol station, where they sold me a flea bomb for £10. Once we had killed the fleas, we divided the work. I took the bathroom, one lad tackled the kitchen, and another the lounge.

The bathroom was unlike anything I had ever seen! The

bath was completely full of faeces, and the toilet was filled to the brim as well. A mountain of tissue, soaked with faeces and bodily fluids, sat beside them. Using gloves and a shovel, I emptied the toilet into a bucket until it was clear enough to clean and get working again. Then, bucket by bucket, I emptied the bath into the toilet until I could clean it properly.

The bed could only be described as resembling the aftermath of the wettest fart imaginable. It had to be disposed of and replaced with a new divan, mattress, and bedding. We cleaned the property and removed every item that couldn't be salvaged. After eliminating the flea infestation, we deep-cleaned the kitchen and lounge, cleaned all carpets and hard flooring, and then sanitised and deodorised the entire place as best as we could.

The staff were amazed when they returned. We had solved so many problems for them! When they asked, "What do we owe you?" I replied, "Is £2,000 okay?"

They said, "Yes, of course!" That was the most money I had ever made in a single day up to that point.

I realised then that I needed training to handle biohazards, pest control, decontamination, and waste properly, as I had guessed my way through it all until that moment!

First Training

I looked everywhere for biohazard training and found a course for death clean-up and body fluid cleaning at the then-called Matthew Bolton College in Birmingham. We were taught by a lady how to clean tomato sauce from a desktop. We were given a piece of paper saying we were now qualified biohazard cleaners. I can't remember the trainer's name, but I remember she wore killer heels! That's about all I remembered from the training, to be honest. What a joke it was! Our trainer had never even seen a death scene, let alone cleaned up the aftermath of anything like what we were about to see during our careers ahead.

I asked one of the lads after the course what they had learned. Their response was priceless:

"Don't eat poo."

What a pointless day! But it gave us a piece of paper that we could show people, proving we were "officially trained." It was after this training that I decided I would start my own training academy and actually teach people how to deal with real-life clean-ups after death and trauma. I will tell you more about that later!

Whenever I am talking to people—whether in the pub or out and about—once they discover my work, I get the usual question:

"What's the worst thing you have ever seen?"

That is a difficult one, as most of them have been pretty horrendous! But there are a few that stick in my memory. Each one is different, as you will see...

His dog ate his leg and face! – My first job after training the team officially

After our terrible training in Birmingham, we advertised with local undertakers, police, solicitors, housing associations, and councils in a bid to get our first job. Within two days, a local solicitor calls us to say that a man has been found in his property. His body had been there for six weeks, and his dog had eaten his face and leg. The dog was still in the property (the RSPCA would meet us at the property to remove the dog), along with piles of dog faeces and body fluid.

The coroner's office or undertaker normally removes the body before we attend. However, on some occasions, the body is still there, and we have to uncover it. I will tell you about one of these situations later.

We drive to a local village, up a farm track, to a discarded farmhouse. All we know is that inside, our careers as biohazard cleaners will begin.

I open the door, and a swarm of bluebottle flies fly straight past my face and out the door. I slam the door shut, wondering if the body might have had a disease or virus like hepatitis B and whether I have now potentially exposed other people to an infectious disease!

"Do flies carry infection?" I wondered. "Why did my training at Matthew Bolton College not cover this?"

"How unprepared for this was I?"

At this point, I have no idea, so at this point—head down and get on with it!

I open the door again. This time, I can clearly smell the odour of rotting body fluid. It is the first time I have ever smelt decomposing human flesh and fluid, and I am taken aback at how strong the smell is!

Nowadays, we have amazing masks that remove malodours, but back then, we could smell most of it through the masks I had purchased, thinking that they would be fine. As I walk closer to the room, I see the decaying matter has soaked through the carpet. I realise how unprepared I am. I have a range of cleaning products and sanitisers that I hope will work, but nothing could prepare me for the amount of effort, energy, and professionalism it would take to clean this property fully.

Donning my white biohazard suit and mask, which I again hope will stop the smell, I enter the room where the body has been. Fortunately, the mask does stop some of the smell, so I am pleased I invested in semi-decent protective equipment and not a mask from the pound shop!

I slowly begin cutting back the carpet, step by step, until a dark sludge stain greets me. This is the man's decomposed body fat. I continue working, spraying, wiping, and bagging as I go. Then I realise that under the carpet is a wooden floor. The body fluid has soaked through this flooring as well.

I have to lift the wooden flooring, and to my surprise, the body fluid has soaked into the concrete beneath. It takes me about two hours to remove the body fat from the concrete floor using only chemicals and products I think will work.

It reminds me of when you cook sausages, then leave the pan to soak in detergent and hot water—the fat breaks up and rises to the surface. Then, you can remove the slurry from the surface. Looking at each other while cleaning, me and the two lads realise this is a crazy job for crazy people. But as we are all nutters, it seems we are made for it. On this job, I just keep seeing £ signs instead of body matter. That helps me keep going.

We do our best: clean everything up, sanitise all we can, remove all the waste, manage to eliminate the odour, and then head home to present the solicitor with an invoice for £2,500. A good day's work for a few crazies.

Until this point, my business was called Ben Giles Cleaning Services. We decide to change it to Ultima Cleaning because, ultimately, we will clean anything!

On site 1 hour after a death

Up until this time, I had only cleaned up areas days after a death had taken place. However, I received a call from a car floor mat manufacturer in the Midlands who needed an urgent clean. As it was, I was already in North Wales pricing some work, so I headed straight to the factory.

I was led to an area in production where a large metal girder had been hit by a reversing forklift truck… and the girder had fallen onto the only person who wasn't wearing a hard hat – the Health and Safety officer!

When I arrived, my view was a large pool of blood, along with loads of paraphernalia left by the paramedics: needles, tubes, gauzes, dressings, etc. To my right-hand side, there was this large yellow girder raised off the floor slightly, with a turban trapped underneath it. The warehouse was empty of workers, and a strange echo accompanied every footstep I made. In the distance, I could see a window with closed blinds where the management usually observed the goings-on.

I hadn't really thought about the person before… it had always been just the mess to clean up. But here, I felt for the man's family and the pain he must have experienced. This girder must have weighed nearly a tonne. The thought of seeing that drop on you? It was horrifying.

It was also strange to be in an environment where everyone viewed me as a professional – like part of the emergency services – even though I was still really new to this. I tried not to be caught like a rabbit in the headlights, not to react like a greenhorn, and to focus on what lay ahead of me.

I cleaned the area, bagged up all the medical gear, and then asked if they wanted me to bag the turban separately for the family – which they did.

I drove back feeling a little empty inside… but also super proud of myself for doing something that others wouldn't or couldn't have done. On my little own, with no one to support or help me!

Blasting the radio with Def Leppard and U2 hits helped me think about anything else on the journey back to West Wales.

Working with the Police

As time passed, and after completing quite a few jobs, we established a really good relationship with our local police authority. We now clean all their cells, vehicles, forensic tents, and any scenes they need us to attend and decontaminate.

Custody cell cleans are eventful! It reminds me of being in a zoo. Some inmates are singing, some are head-butting the metal door, some are shouting, some are being searched internally, some are crying, and some are sleeping it off!

We get a whole cocktail of body fluids: blood, vomit, urine, semen, faeces, and a whole array of infestations and bacterial or virucidal infections that require decontamination.

Most cells are just a bit of blood here and there from a nosebleed, or some spit on the walls… along with the common toilet roll soaked in water and thrown at the ceiling—especially the camera! But some are more interesting.

Once, very early in my career as a crime scene cleaner, I was asked to clean a cell. I think the prisoner had scabies, and I was asked to decontaminate it. As I walked past an occupied cell en route to the empty one I had to clean, I noticed a small mesh grid allowing airflow into the cell. My shadow, or the noise of me putting on my white suit outside the mesh, must have alerted the prisoner that I was there.

He said, “Who’s there?”

I stupidly replied, “I am just cleaning a cell.”

When I say "stupidly," I mean it was foolish of me to engage in conversation with a nutter! It was quite unnerving for me, as a greenhorn, to be told next:

“I am going to kill you and your family. I will rape your missus and burn your house down.”

Oh, my days! It really shook me up—firstly, because I wasn’t expecting it, and second, because I had never met anyone who would say anything like that to a stranger! I learned quickly not to engage with any prisoners in there, and my respect for the custody team grew immensely, realising that was just one thing they encounter on almost a daily basis!

I also managed to lock myself in a cell for 30 minutes! Not realising that if I closed the door without asking a custody officer to unlock it beforehand, I'd be stuck. That got a laugh from the officers watching me on the security cameras as I waved my hands and shouted for help! Again, a rookie mistake I didn't make again.

Some cells are pretty difficult to clean, especially if the prisoner has had diarrhoea down the door and it's run under the door and out into the hallway. You can't just lift the door off, so you have to use a scissor action with a cloth under the door to remove the poo from the underside of the door. It's especially lovely when a piece of sweetcorn emerges!

I have had cells where a female prisoner has been arrested and there's a cocktail of faeces, urine, vomit, and blood smeared all over the walls and floor. Others where I am convinced they'd arrested a whale—as there was so much semen all over the walls! And then there are hundreds of cells where there have been dirty protests, where a prisoner has spread his faeces all over the cell, pushed it into every nook and cranny, door crack, inspection window, and also all over themselves!

In a hope not to go to court, some literally cover themselves in their own excrement, but a hose-down in the exercise yard or a few minutes under the shower ensures their inevitable magistrate appearance always happens.

Then there are the really weird ones—like when a person

is arrested and decides to sit in their cell and eat their own excrement, completing the occasional finger painting on the wall at the same time! Don't ask me why they do it—I have no idea.

Being asked to decontaminate a cell after the deployment of pepper spray was an interesting one! And also being asked to remove cocaine from the back seat of a police car was a first for me… Try finding a method for that on Google that doesn't involve rolling up a fiver and snorting it! But we managed to create methods, design chemicals, and even built training manuals… which stood us in good stead for future work and training others.

There isn't really much money in decontaminating custody cells and police vehicles… But it's been a great way to build a relationship with police forces and has opened up lots of doors to crime scene cleaning, forensic equipment cleaning, specialist suites for victims of rape, etc.

There are also forensic chemicals that we had to learn how to remove: ninhydrin, luminol, Amido Black, etc. None of these chemicals had ever had any specific method of removal, or a designated chemical designed to remove them from surfaces… So, I set about working with a chemist and creating our own specialist cleaning products that we now sell online under our own branding.

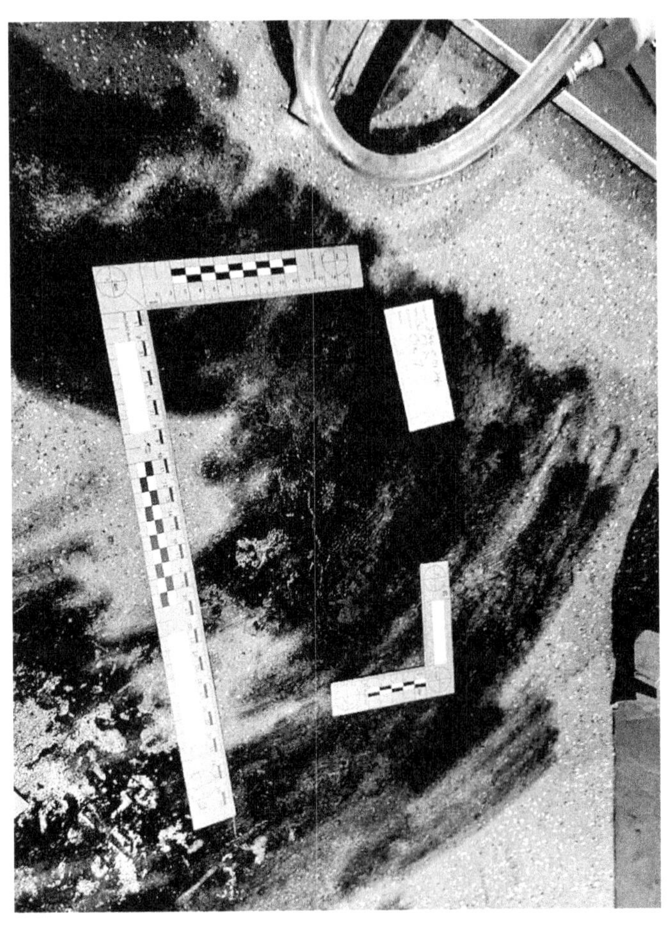

Roads and Highways

Normally, when you see a van on the road with "motorway maintenance" or "highway maintenance" in reflective stickers go past, your last thought is probably that they may have just cleaned up the remains of someone off the tarmac! But with over 1,700 fatalities a year on UK roads, it's a common thing for us to deal with. Not just vehicle accidents, but many suicides off bridges and structures along the roads as well.

Normally, the council closes the roads off and the police carry out all the investigations they need to determine liability and cause of death. Then we are asked to come in and clean down... There can be a mix of oil and blood, body parts, and vehicle debris to sort through. Any body parts retrieved are bagged and given over to the coroner's office to be repatriated to the body, and then all the blood and fallout needs to be sanitised and removed.

It's a little-known fact that Hepatitis B can survive for up to eight weeks in water... This means that we have to be meticulous about any runoff into drains, using absorbent and drain covers if close by.

It's also interesting who pays the bill for the cleanup on roads... Normally, in an accident, the driver at fault's insurance company pays for everything: the recovery, repairs to roads, and even the clean-up!

Motorbike accidents are particularly harrowing to clean up, as there is normally high speed involved and the fallout can be difficult, with personal clothing and biker's gear to collect and clean. We have been asked to clean motorcycle helmets that are soaked in blood and dented heavily for the family to have at the funeral – this is extremely sensitive, and we go to every effort to clean and restore the helmet with the help of a mate who is a car body repair guy, and hand it back to the family looking like new to sit on the coffin. Again, an immense amount of pride is felt by all when the family is so grateful for all our efforts.

We also have to clean up animals that have died in accidents, being carried in trailers or lorries, and roadkill in some cases. Memorable ones include an artic lorry full of pig skin and fat that shed its load, and a trailer full of sheep on the M4 that collided with a bin lorry. A train that hit 60 sheep on the track at high speed! We have some specialist partners who deal with the removal of the animal carcasses, and we deal with all the leftover stuff. I once got asked to go to a railway workshop where a train had hit a person who jumped in front of it. The place was dirty and oily and just normally used to service the diesel engines. There stood the train waiting for me, blood all over the glass and the front nose, flesh caught in cracks and crevices. After cleaning down the front of the train, I jet-washed the underside and, to my horror, a wrist and hand fell from under the skirt of the train! I notified the police and this was collected and removed. Although unprepared to see that, I managed to cope with collecting it and putting it into a bag, and again left feeling that I had completed a task many others would not even think about, let alone carry out.

Uncovering a body that's been under rubbish for 10 weeks.

I received a call from the coroner's office who said they wanted our help with a body clean-up. The trouble was, the mackerel were in the bay! Me, Rod, and Joe were supposed to be going fishing that day on the boat. I told Rod that we'd probably still be able to go fishing, and he said he'd help me get the job done faster. I asked Joe if he'd help, and he said no. I offered him £100, he said no. £200, he said no. £400, he said yes! When I went to pick Rod up, he was holding a pair of Crocs in his hands and said, "Will these do?" "No, mate!" I said, and he grabbed his wellies.

When we arrived at the estate, about sixty people were there watching, along with the police and fire brigade. The police asked me if I could locate the body, as the property was lived in by a hoarder. So, the police forced the door, and I was met by a tunnel surrounded by suitcases and boxes. I crawled in and followed the tunnel, lined by boxes and video cassettes, up the stairs, not seeing any doors or entrances. Up I went, and I came to a door—that was the first time I could stand up. The door had been barricaded from the inside. I could smell the body decaying inside.

I crawled back down the stairs and out of the tunnel and explained to the police officer that I couldn't get to the body. The fire brigade was asked to break the window of the barricaded room where the body was. We waited near the van and started to suit up. Joe and Rod had no clue what they were going to do or see! It didn't help when a fireman returned from breaking the window with tears running down his face, crying, and put his hand on Joe's shoulder and said, "I wouldn't want your job." Joe looked at me and said, "He sees blood and death every day... What is so bad that he wouldn't want my job?" I tried to reassure him that it must have been his first day.

But then, all the sixty people watching began to run to their houses as the odour of decaying body matter hit the street from the broken window! Me, Joe, and Rod walked up to the house now wearing our Cat 3 suits and A1P2 masks, which stop 100% of the smell! I climbed the firefighter's ladder and stepped onto the windowsill and into the room. The room was full, up to the windowsill, with collections of old boxes, video tapes in bundles of fifties, suitcases and bags and bags of stuff the guy had hoarded. Joe stood on the ladder outside the window waiting to receive the first bag of waste from me, and Rod was below in the garden ready to receive the waste from Joe.

I started to bag up waste, knowing that sooner or later, I'd reach the corpse. After bagging about 20 bags of dry waste, I came across a leg—well, it was a bone wrapped in withered, brown, leathery skin. I moved another bag, and his foot came off! After putting his foot back into position, I motioned to Joe to come inside. "There's his leg," I said. Joe, trying to focus on the area I was pointing to, said, "Where?" "There," I said, pointing to the bone.

Joe looked at me and said, "What's the best holiday you've ever been on?" I said, "What?" He said, "Just talk about anything… PLEASE." I said, "Thailand… now get a grip! The area you're going to dig in is where his head will be." Joe started digging and bagging and then came across the head, eyes sunken in, a neat beard, and the same brown leathery skin wrapped around it. He looked at me and said, "It looks kind of cute." Weird!!

When we had exposed the whole body, we called the police over and asked them what they wanted to do now that we had exposed the corpse. They sent a young female SOCO up the ladder to take a picture, wearing a white suit and a pathetic dust mask. You could see the grimace on her face as she inhaled the foul aroma and then started to hold back from retching. She took a few pictures and descended the ladder. Next came the hilarious bit when two doctors climbed the ladder to certify that the man was, in fact, dead! The recent Harold Shipman case meant that two doctors had to pronounce a body deceased. Where they were going to put his stethoscope, I have no idea!

We then stepped back and allowed the undertakers to enter and bag up what was left of the body. We were then called in again to start removing the waste in the room—three mattresses stacked on top of each other, all soaked in body fluid and decomposed fat. In total, 4.2 tonnes of waste... from one room!

When we were finished, I asked Rod and Joe if they still wanted to go fishing. "Definitely," was the answer. So we rushed home, stopping at two petrol stations to buy bottles of Febreze air freshener to spray ourselves down! Fishing was good, and the day was ended by Joe sending me a text saying that his wife, who was vegetarian, had decided to cook him a lamb shank for tea. "The meat was falling off the bone," the text said!! Poor bloke!!

A family dog mauled a young baby

These are particularly difficult scenes to clean, where you can normally turn up with a sign-written van saying “biohazard cleaner” and walk in wearing your gear because everyone knows what has happened. But these events are kept quiet from the public for as long as possible to protect the family. In all the cases I’ve worked, the family has been in the house, often in another room. I’ve heard crying and shouting from family members, and I can’t imagine how traumatic it must be to have a family pet take the life of your child. With the new laws on keeping dangerous dogs, I suppose this may be something less common nowadays.

It’s a truly sensitive place to be and one that requires serious forethought about what needs to be done. You can’t be asking questions like, “Do you want me to throw away the cot bedding and toys that are contaminated?” at the scene. A long talk with a family liaison officer beforehand is crucial, so all information is clear and you’re prepared to enter, decontaminate, and leave as politely and courteously as possible. The goal is to ensure that you leave no issues behind that will make their lives harder or more complicated at that moment. It’s a strange thing, really, to have a career that is fuelled by what is probably the worst timing in people’s lives.

A local seamstress

So, the phone rings… The head of Dyfed Powys Police's forensic team asks us to attend a property about thirty minutes away. We had heard previously there had been a murder. Mark and I head out. We meet the forensic officer, and he unlocks the door. We enter to see forensic stickers and markers on the carpet. We begin working our way into the lounge, where only a few drops of blood are circled by marker pen, and everything looks in its place. But as we move into the kitchen, we're met with a scene where a fight has clearly taken place. Black powder has been used to stabilise the blood and to clearly define both a bare footprint and that of a shoe. Blood is splattered across the floor, walls, over the worktops, door handles, and even inside the kitchen cupboards.

Forensics quickly worked out what had happened. There were clearly two different sets of footsteps, and bloodied fingerprints on the window blinds where the murderer had shut them.

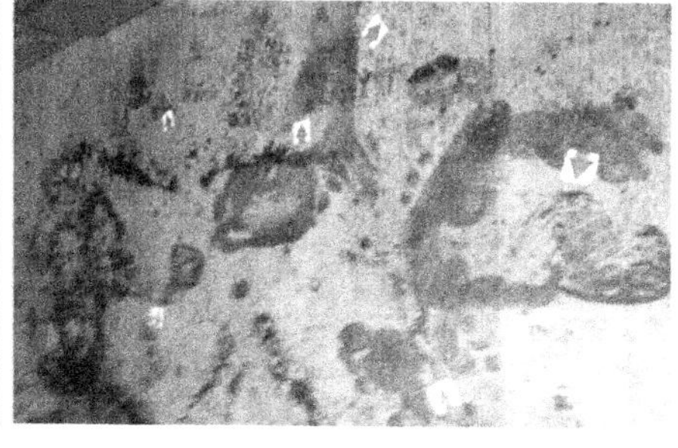

As we start to work our way into the kitchen, cleaning as we go, we see the full extent of the violence that has taken place. Blood isn't just on the kitchen cupboards—it's been sprayed into the kitchen drawers and even underneath them, meaning we have to empty the entire kitchen to clean and sanitise.

The washing machine is covered in blood that has run down the front and seeped behind the door seal. There's also blood on top, in the gap between the underside of the worktop and the top of the washing machine. I often wonder what happened in the struggle when I see such evidence of brutal violence.

On the floor, there's an outline of a person's back in blood. Even the blood-soaked jumper the victim was wearing has left a clear outline under the table where she must have collapsed. As I clean this up, I look under the table and once again find a fine mist of red spray that will need to be removed.

Mark continues to clean off forensic stickers on light switches and the odd circular marker pen outlines around drops of blood on the floor. Except for a quick double-check, we meet at the kitchen doorway, having quietly done what was needed. We're ready to head home, seemingly unaffected, but our hearts go out to that poor lady and what she went through the day before.

I'm still puzzled at how animalistic humans can be towards one another. Why would someone do this to another person? How does someone cross that line and commit murder? What makes it worse is that the murderer was arrested in the local pub. After committing such a heinous act, he was composed enough to walk into the local and have a drink with others, while his wife lay dead in her house. How do people do that?

Like you, I've probably seen crime scene documentaries where the killer has even helped officers look for the person they killed as part of a community-led search, only to later be convicted of the murder! What goes through a person's mind and conscience that allows them to do this?

The table saw

A call comes in from a North Wales police force — a man has committed suicide, and a clean-up is required. We ask, “What happened?”, “What’s the scene like?”

The reply makes you sit down. We hear that a father attended court that day and lost the battle for custody of his son. Emotionally charged and aware that everything that once mattered to him now seems lost, he steps into his garage, undoes the two bolts holding the protective guard over the 15" blade on his table saw, turns on the power, and drops his throat onto the spinning blade.

I turn to Pete and say, "We need to discuss this one... who do we send?"

Ian and Johnny are chosen, due to their experience, and we call them in to discuss the clean-up required. Ian, an amazing father of four, immediately says, "I don't think I can do this one." I agree and say, "Mate, I realise that as a dad this is really hard, I’ll find someone else." But he then says, "I’ll try. If I can’t, can you sort another?" Of course, I say yes. After loading up the van, off they go.

We get a call when they are there, saying how bad it is: blood on the floor, walls, and ceiling; flesh scattered all over tools and items in the garage. A line of blood and flesh can be seen from the saw blade across the floor, up the wall, and along the ceiling. There’s loads of waste to remove, and a complicated clean-up required on the table saw. Instructions are given, and they work their way into the room, cleaning up and sanitising as they go.

About six hours later, they return. Both are pretty silent on the return journey, having worked incredibly hard and been exceptionally professional.

But as they unload all the bags of waste and share images of the clean, all of us take a minute to reflect on what that man must have gone through. We all think about how valuable our families are to us. My staff are amazing. Truly amazing.

Elderly man and the angle grinder.

This scene stands out as particularly harrowing for me. It's not often we get to know all the facts, but sadly, this gentleman had been married to his childhood sweetheart since they were 18 years old. Now well into his seventies, he suffered from dementia and depression. His wife, who had been his carer, left him asleep in an armchair while she nipped up to the shop to grab a few items.

When she returned about thirty minutes later, she found that he had gone into the garage and tried to take his own life with an angle grinder. Sadly, or perhaps fortunately—I'm still not sure—he missed his jugular vein and instead cut open his throat, destroying his voice box. He survived, but he was in an awful state.

The fallout from the angle grinder was horrific—flesh and blood spattered all over the garage walls, floors, and ceiling. Every single item had to be meticulously cleaned and sanitised, from the hand tools to the ceilings and walls. As we worked, I couldn't help but feel an overwhelming sense of sympathy for him and his poor wife. I can't imagine what it must be like for them to cope with something so traumatic at their age.

Thousands of needles to collect

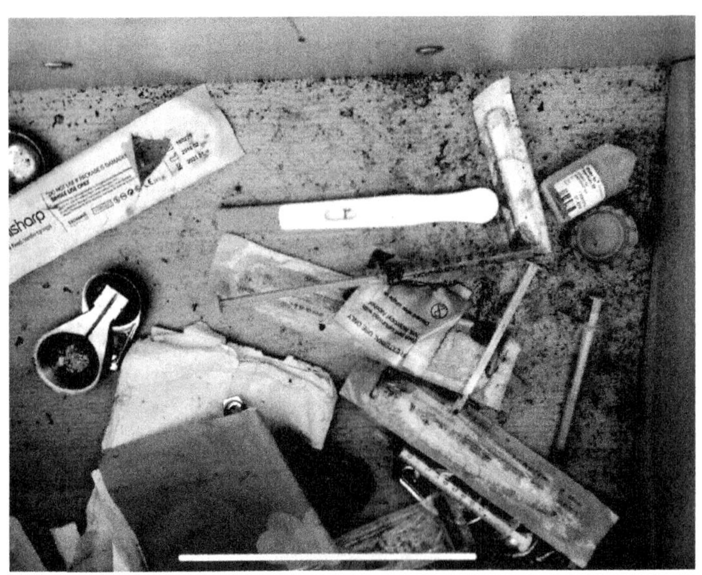

A call from a construction company comes in; they are due to start work on a disused, listed building at Bath train station. When they removed the boarding from the windows, needles could be seen – hence the phone call to us.

We attend the site to find a very old, beautiful building, I believe Victorian, boarded up, with the garden lined by large oak trees. There is Herras fencing to the inside of the tree line all the way around the property. On hand is a structural engineer in his tweed jacket, glasses, and corduroy trousers. He asks why we are there, and we say to remove the needles from the property. I ask why he is here – he says, "I'm a structural engineer and I have to make sure it's safe for you to go in."

As we remove the boarding from the front door and open the door, we are greeted with a syringe on the floor mat. The intelligent, corduroy- and tweed-wearing man looks to me and says, "I can't go in if there are needles in there!" I say, "I'm not supposed to go in there unless you say it's safe." So, here's the dilemma – if neither of us can go in, how on earth are we going to get this job done?!

I decide to nip off and get some crawling boards from a local hire company and start working my way in as the structural engineer returns to his BMW and drives back to his office. Working our way through the building, a team of three of us manage to collect roughly 6,000 used hypodermic needles from floors, cracks in tiles, worktops, and underneath furniture. The musty smell of a disused property reminds us of so many of these jobs we've done before. After about three hours and a complete search and double-check of every room, we are told that the company is happy to sign the building off.

Just as we are about to leave, we're asked to come back as they have now found a basement underneath the building with a small entrance onto the garden behind. So, off we go to get some temporary lighting from the hire shop and determine the safe method to work in a basement surrounded by hundreds of needles.

When a decision is made, we head back, set up the lights, and start to work our way into the building. Little did we know how dangerous this was to become – with the sound of the generator in the background powering our festoon of lights, coupled with white suits and masks reducing many of our senses, we enter this soot-filled basement where someone has been burning items to stay warm and a massive collection of drug paraphernalia where addicts have been shooting up. Working our way in – we begin collecting needle after needle after needle.

After about 20 minutes of work, I turn around and, to my horror, 5 feet in front of me is a drug addict injecting into his wrist right next to me. I don't know what to do – whether to alert the rest of the crew but risk panicking them, or whether to approach the addict standing next to me and ask him to leave, knowing he's off his face on drugs. So, I decide to gently walk towards one of my team and tap them on the shoulder, then point towards the drug addict and take them to one side where it is safer. I then move to the next member of the team and do the same.

We stop work, staring at the drug addict who turns around, throws his used needle on the floor, looks at us, smiles, and gently makes his way out of the basement.

We all realise how crazy this could've become if things had just been slightly different. Next, we have to work out how this has happened with 8-foot Harris fencing surrounding the entire site. But with one glance, it becomes totally evident that the Harris fencing has been placed inside the tree line by the construction company, instead of outside, meaning that the drug addict could easily just climb a tree and jump straight into the area we were working in. Even worse, now he is trapped inside the makeshift compound and starts to panic, looking for an exit! We manage to run up the fence line to the gate and open it for him to leave, shouting to him that this is the way out! He leaves with no issues.

But this is a mistake that we will never make again. Never will we allow others to close off an area without checking first! Why did he come back, you may ask? Well, his stash of drugs was also in the basement! Thank goodness we got away with this one.

I love the expression: "Experience is what you get when you didn't get what you wanted." We certainly gained a lot of experience on that job!

Frozen Peas, chips, a knife and suicide notes

One of the most bizarre and haunting forms of suicide, to me, is disembowelling. I truly can't fathom what must be going through someone's mind to choose such a method, to inflict such pain upon themselves. The thought of cutting myself is enough to make me shudder, let alone using a knife to cut through my stomach, organs, and intestines. Even writing this makes me uneasy. Tragically, many people do choose this method, and the aftermath can be harrowing to witness.

I've entered properties where the floor and bed are covered in blood and bowel fluid, but

in some cases, I've also found frozen peas, chips, and

vegetables scattered around. At first, I was puzzled by this, but it soon became clear—during their immense pain, the individual had likely grabbed anything cold and frozen to try to numb the injury. The thought of that still disturbs me.

Over the years, I've cleaned up from many disembowelment suicides. Some have been particularly difficult. One case stands out, where a gentleman had not only disembowelled himself but, for some unknown reason, used a pair of scissors to snip pieces of his intestines off and toss them into the bath. I can't explain why anyone would do this, but it meant that in addition to cleaning the wound area, we had to remove the intestines and the scissors from the bath.

Another memorable job involved a person who had used a razor blade to cut themselves open. The blade was still there, and when they cut themselves in the shower, the mixture of body fluids and bowel material blocked the drain. We ended up having to buy a bottle of Mr. Muscle drain unblocker to clear the pipes. That job taught me a hard lesson. I once neglected to check a drain after cleaning a property where someone had bled out in a sink. The property manager called me back to check on the sink, and when I turned on the water, it drained fine. But then the shower and bath began to fill with red water, indicating that the pipes in the trap had been blocked lower down. I was so grateful I hadn't handed the keys to a family member—the emotional trauma they would have experienced could have been unbearable. It was a crucial lesson I'll never forget, and one I now pass along to new recruits.

Surprisingly, I've attended a few cases where the person survived. The aftermath of such a traumatic act is difficult to imagine, and the physical damage they must have inflicted upon themselves is horrific. One police officer shared a story with us after we cleaned a static caravan where someone had attempted suicide by disembowelling. After cutting themselves open, they climbed into bed. The angle at which they lay seemed to close the wound, and when they woke up in the morning, they were alive. They called an ambulance for help, and as far as I know, they survived.

These experiences are incredibly tough to process, but they also highlight the importance of the work we do, the lessons we learn, and the strength required to face such traumatic scenes head-on.

Sadly, another one I attended where the person survived also...

We were called back to the same property about eight years later to more or less exactly the same scene. It puzzled me, as when my team showed me the photos, I said, "I cleaned

that up years ago!"

They said, "No, it was the same guy, and he had done it again!"

This time, sadly, he had passed away. Why someone would want to try this twice is beyond me. What must be going through their minds to inflict so much pain? Truly saddening to think about.

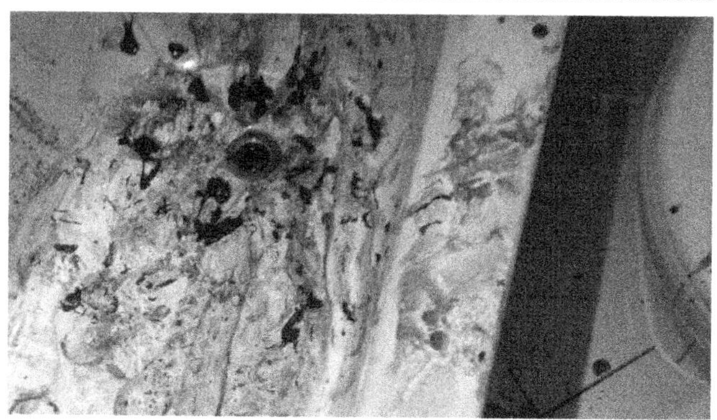

I am always looking for an opportunity, and on one job, which was where somebody had disembowelled themselves in a static caravan, a bizarre opportunity showed itself. We had the call from the environmental health department, who instructed us to go and clean a static caravan that somebody was living in permanently.

Again, the fallout was awful—body fluid right through the caravan, the hardboard walls saturated in blood, the mattress and bedding totally soaked. After working all morning removing all of the contaminated material, cutting away hardboard walls, sanitising and decontaminating surfaces, the caravan was finally in a position for the environmental health officer to call in and see us.

I asked, "What is happening to the caravan?" She said, "We're going to sell it to pay your bill!" My mind started to see an opportunity, and I asked, "Can I take the caravan as payment for my work?"

With a phone call made, the answer was yes. I would normally have charged about £1200 for that job, so I was hoping that the caravan was worth more. The only caveat was that the caravan had to be removed within two days.

My parents have a holiday complex and used to have static caravans, so I called my dad and asked him if he could get in touch with the guys from Ireland who used to buy his second-hand caravans. I gave him the make and the model and took photos of the damage we had made to it by removing hardboard walls and some of the fixed furniture, hoping that the value would be worth more than £1200!

Dad called me back within half an hour and said, "They will give you £6000 for it, and they can collect it the next day!"

I decided to surprise my wife that weekend, along with two friends, with an amazing trip to a plush hotel to reward myself for my ingenuity! The fact was, though, that it could have gone horribly wrong! I guess it's instances like this that have made me happy to take risks. These days, I'm willing to have a bash at almost anything!

Natural and undiscovered death scenes

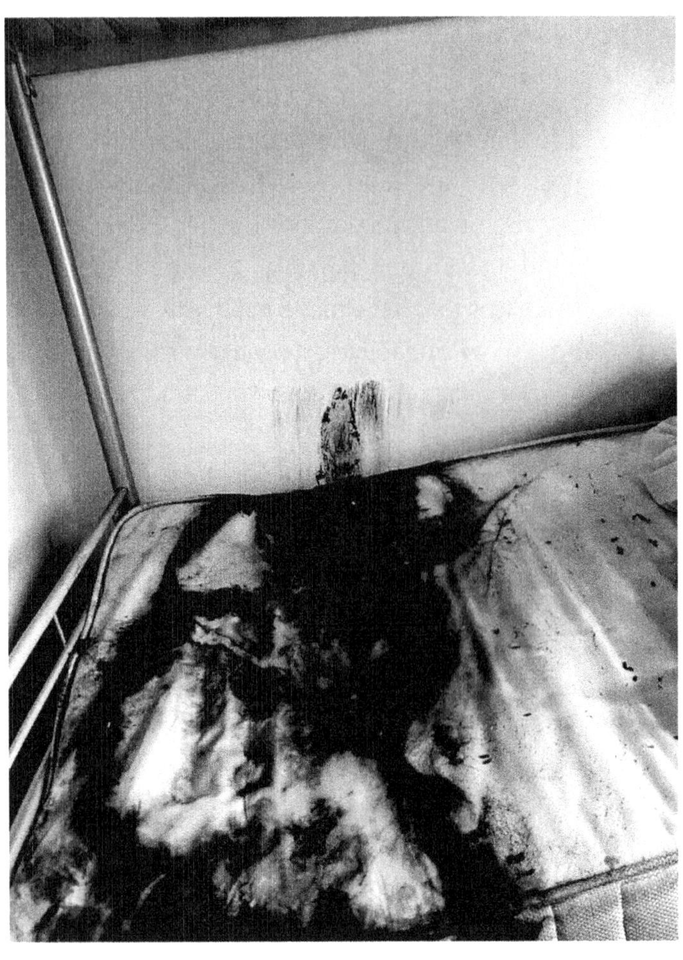

The longer a body is in a property undiscovered, the worse pretty much the whole job is. The police refer to these as natural deaths—and they can be undiscovered for long periods of time. There are some bizarre incidents here also.

One time, one of our teams attended a job with an undertaker, and the body had been in the property undiscovered for fifteen years! As they climbed over the junk mail behind the door and walked into the lounge, they found a skeleton with a leather belt intact and leather shoes still on its skeletal feet!

"How," you ask, "does this happen?"

Well, when families move away, disputes happen, or families simply stop looking out for each other. When all bills are paid by direct debit and friends are no longer present, it's a sad fact that people can die alone.

I suppose seeing this first-hand has made me determined to ensure I don't fall out with family. No matter what happens, I always try to make up, restore bonds, and reassure my family that I'm there for them. My family is amazing—so it's easier for me to be great friends with them.

I once got asked to attend a property for an estate agent in London. They wanted the property next door to the estate agent's office cleaned out. Apparently, the owner, a Turkish man, had just up and left for Turkey. They bad-mouthed him, explaining that he had left no trace, left loads of bills unpaid, had no thought for anyone, and that the place was dirty and smelt awful. Finally, after months and months of legal work, the owner of the house had regained possession and wanted it emptied.

I collected the keys and went next door to start clearing out and deodorising. As I entered the first floor, I could smell decomposed body matter. Thinking I was going to find a pet cat or dog possibly in a corner, I approached a dark staircase leading to the basement. I grabbed a torch (the electricity supply had been cut off as he hadn't paid any bills before running off to Turkey, apparently). There was something at the base of the staircase.

As I walked down, I realised it was the Turkish man. The poor guy had fallen down the stairs over twelve months ago! Work stopped immediately. I went into the estate agent's and explained that they were wrong about the owner fleeing. One lady in the office asked, "He's not still there, is he?"

I said, "Yes, but sadly, I think he fell to his death months ago."

The police were called, and the job was aborted for the time being. I did hope he had died quickly. The thought of him being there on his own, in pain, again played on my mind.

One massive factor in the clean-up following a decomposition is the weight of the person. You would expect the scene to always smell horrendous. However, I have cleaned up scenes where elderly people, who must have weighed hardly anything, had died naturally on a mattress. All there was to do was bag the mattress and sanitise the area—no smell and no major body fluid fallout.

However, I have also cleaned up after some really fat people who had decomposed. Sometimes the decomposition saturated entire sofas, mattresses, divans, wooden flooring, carpeting, and, as mentioned, even soaked into concrete floors.

I once cleaned a house as a freebie—it was for a friend I met through giving college lectures on self-employment. Her ex-husband sadly took his own life in the loft of a house and had been there for weeks. His decomposed body fluid had run through the loft, down through the first-floor ceiling. Fluid often finds the easiest route, like electric cables, pipework, ceiling lights, etc. It had dropped through the light pendant onto the first floor and then through the first floor, puddling on the hallway floor on the ground floor. A major clean-up was required, and the whole property needed deodorising and sanitising.

Not to forget, there are the infestations at decomposing scenes—normally hundreds of blowflies (blue bottles and green bottles), along with their larvae. Thousands of maggots eat up all the decomposed matter and head off to find darkness to pupate and metamorphose into flies again, repeating the cycle until there's no matter left to eat. There is also the chance of some skin beetles if the body has been outside for some time following death.

I had to learn all of this to deal with infestations, and this also became part of our training course to help new recruits learn how to deal with them.

I remember a property that I went to; this was in West Wales. We had been told that the lady often took last-minute holidays, and the fact that her children could not get hold of her was a common occurrence because she had just grabbed a last-minute flight and was overseas somewhere, having the time of her life.

I had to learn all of this to deal with infestations, and this also became part of our training course to help new recruits learn how to deal with them.

I remember a property that I went to; this was in West Wales. We had been told that the lady often took last-minute holidays, and the fact that her children could not get hold of her was a common occurrence because she had just grabbed a last-minute flight and was overseas somewhere, having the time of her life.

Sadly, in this instance, this was not the case. Following a heart attack, she had sadly passed away some six weeks before and was on the floor in her bedroom.

When I initially went into the room, it was so dark that I didn't realise there was a Velux window in the bedroom. This was because, as I later realised, it was about two inches deep in bluebottles trying to get out of the room. It was probably one of the worst infestations I've seen.

I also remember that in this property, I learned an important lesson: never trust that a floor is level! As I walked into the room, although I was at least 20 feet away from where the body had been, I immediately felt squelching underfoot in the carpet beneath me. I later realised that under the carpet was an old vinyl floor, and the floor was sloping towards the doorway.

All her body fluid had been running under the carpet towards the door, and I had inadvertently stepped in it all! Having to walk backwards, find a safe place to clean myself down—including my boots—and start again, working my way in, was a mistake I never made again.

Treating the fly infestation is a choice of two options, really. Either let them all out by opening the windows—not an option if you are close to neighbours, as the smell is horrendous and not fair to share with them—or set off a smoke generator.

This emits a cloud of pesticide that, as it's hot, stays up in the air. As the flies fly through the smoke, they get the pesticide on them and fall to the ground. As the nerve agent makes contact, they begin that weird breakdance move, spinning on their backs.

Normally, this isn't an issue, but the noise from literally thousands of flies all spinning and going crazy is a weird thing to behold!

One of my first natural death scenes was a decomposition, where the gentleman had died and been on the floor next to his bed on the first floor, decomposing for 6-8 weeks. This was in the Bristol area. His body fluid had saturated the carpet, the chipboard furniture,

and the MDF skirting board. Under the carpet, we found saturated chipboard flooring, which we had to remove as well. I remember hearing the maggots eating in the middle of the goo that was his remains, like the sound you hear when you push saliva in and out of your teeth with your mouth closed – it was that noise!

On this one, his two sons met us there. And here was the first time I remembered having to use my customer relations skills. One of the sons said, "Thanks so much for coming to clean up the remains of their father," crying. I expressed my deepest sympathy for their loss, explained we would do our very best to remove anything that would cause any trauma to them, and I also asked one of the sons where he had travelled from, only to be told, "I live at the bottom of the road."

I thought to myself, "He's been here for up to 8 weeks dead, and he lives a stone's throw away… how sad?" Then came the question from one of the sons: "When do you think it is likely that an estate agent could look around the property?" It became very clear what was wanted.

I said I could, on top of the clean-up, replace the flooring and skirting, install new carpet, and repaint the walls by the end of the day if they were willing to pay for it. "YES," came the reply, "that would be amazing!" So we replaced all the flooring and skirting with new materials from Jewson builders' merchants, but I am no carpet fitter!

I searched locally for a carpet fitter and asked if he could fit a new carpet in a bedroom – just a plain biscuit colour. He said, "No problem, would be £140 with the measurements I gave him." I asked, "Can you fit today?" "No chance!" was the reply. I said, "I would pay you £250 instead… any chance?" "No," came the reply. "£350?" I said. "Sorry, no," was the reply. "£450?" "I'll be there in 1 hour!"

So we left the property ready to be put on the market the

same day and walked away with

£5,000!

I remember a film crew asking to follow us for a series they were putting together on extreme cleaning. Most jobs we asked if we could film – the answer was an immediate no, totally understandable. But one family, who were overseas, agreed to allow us to film the clean-up of their auntie's property in London. I made the film crew wear suits, masks, and even get tetanus inoculations. I sat them down and explained that the body had been there for six weeks and that the smell would be horrendous!

As we opened the door and walked into the bedroom, there was no smell at all! A simple outline, like a water mark on the mattress, and no fallout at all! It was then that I realised this poor woman had sadly been just a few stones in weight when she died, zero body fat, and so there was nothing to clean – just slide the mattress into a mattress bag and walk away with it! A bit of a letdown for the film crew, who were expecting horrendous conditions after my build-up!

The smell!! Ok, this is probably most people's fear – and if you can't handle terrible smells, this certainly isn't the job for you! You may say, "Don't the masks you wear remove the smell?" … Yes, they do, until you take your mask off and the outside of the mask and filters release the odour of death! What's it like? Well, that's a difficult thing to explain... smells are difficult to explain anyway! Like, what's the worst fart you have ever smelt?

But something that happened to me in Surinam, believe it or not, was quite strange and related to the decomposition smell. There I was, sitting in a Thai restaurant with my family and friends, as we were visiting... and my food arrived with a sauce poured over it. The sauce was created by rotting fish over stones and collecting the juice that ran through the stones. Almost vomiting, this was the first time I had ever associated the smell of decomposition with food!! It wasn't helped when later that night my good friend, for a prank, poured me a whisky over ice. As I drank it, I realised he had pranked me with rotting fish sauce!! A night throwing up ensued!

Very often, we have to empty old fridges and freezers that are full of rotting food, also where power has been turned off due to a trauma. When it comes to hoarder cleans, we sometimes have to remove hundreds of bottles of stagnant urine or kilos of human faeces wrapped up in newspaper in freezers, or empty bathtubs brimming with urine and fences with a crust on it that, when broken through, is horrendous!

One job we were asked to attend was like this – a property in Pembrokeshire where the lady who lived there needed an environmental clean, we were told. We arrived and were greeted by the environmental health team, who had served the enforcement notice on the house. The lady wasn't there, so we had to wait as she travelled home from work. She arrived and was about 25 stone. She said hello and opened up her front door for us all to enter.

As I walked in behind the officer, I realised that after the first few steps, I was not walking uphill! And sure enough, in her lounge, the depth of rubbish was so much that my head hit the ceiling! I had to limbo past the light and walk back down the other side into the kitchen! The kitchen had the usual pyramid, about 1 foot high, of teabags and a pile of eggshells that were stuck together with the waste bit of egg that never comes out when you crack it. The pile was about 3 feet high and 2 feet wide! I thought for a moment that some of these sculptures, rubbish piles, would look fine in the Tate Modern!

The officer said, "The best bit is yet to come." As we walked into the bathroom, the bath was full to the brim with poo, the toilet was not only full but had a pyramid of poo out of the top, looking like Mount Fuji! And the floor was about two feet deep in used toilet paper!

A first for me was that she had sat on the loo and compressed the poo so much that it had actually gone up the flush pipe and into the cistern above! I suppose 25 stone will do that!

At that point, Johnny, one of our staff who is an absolute legend, appeared and asked, "What's first?" I said, "Can we get the toilet out and remove the waste, as we can't clean it?" Johnny replied, "I can clean that!"

He left and came back with a ladle and a bucket and immediately broke the crust of the pyramid! With no mask on, as we weren't really prepared for Johnny's eagerness, we started wrenching, our eyes watering from the rank smell and ammonia that was released! Johnny, who has no sense of smell, laughed at us and called us a bunch of pussies as we ran out of the room!

We found the outdoor sewer manhole, and Johnny proceeded to wash all the years of poop down the drain! In all fairness to him, he brought the loo back to life! When the loo was working and the cistern free of poo, we could start to empty the contents of the bath down the loo. (I have paid Porta Loo companies to come and empty baths full of poo for us in the past – that works also.)

What was strange on the scene was, after we had removed all the loo paper, about 200 kg of poo, and all the waste from the kitchen and the lounge (we were never allowed in the bedroom – goodness knows what delights were in there!), the owner came up to us and said, "Thanks, sorry I was late, I had a long shift at work." I said, “No bother,” but intrigued, I asked what she did for work. Her reply knocked me sideways: “I am a nurse at the local hospital.”

Oh my days! What sort of infection could have been passed on by her? And I suppose it’s these facts that make this job surreal at times. Just normal people you interact with on a daily basis lead some crazy lives! Like cat women (I call them that) – jobs where usually a woman has sometimes 30-50 cats living in her house, and one or two rooms are up to a foot deep in faeces – a giant litter tray! I will talk about these amazing people later on!

I got asked to clean up a natural death with a bit of a twist in Cornwall. The call came in from an insurance company, where they had paid a few companies to go and try to clean up and remove the smell in the property. The owner of the property, who had been renting it to the previous tenants, refused to accept the property back from the insurance company because the smell was so bad. All we had been told was that somebody had died in the property and that after three or four attempts to clean it, the foul stench still lingered.

After doing a little digging with the neighbours and asking what had happened, they told me that somebody had passed away in the property but had fallen onto a three-bar fire. The old electric fires were three glowing hot bars that ran through them. The person had not caught fire, but a lot of the body matter had evaporated into the air in the property.

After opening the door, I could immediately smell decomposed body matter, but I could also smell a weird burning scent that went along with it. It was strange, but I could only relate it to one time when I cooked a stew and forgot to turn it off, and it boiled dry. The grease and smell managed to get onto almost everything in the room. This property was no different.

Where the body had been on the floor over the fire, there was a stain in the concrete. I had to use a bolster and hammer to remove the concrete, which revealed a block and beam floor underneath. Lifting the blocks, I found a puddle of residue underneath, but it had soaked into some shale under the house. After removing the contaminated material, I replaced the blocks and, after nipping to the local builders' merchants, bought some concrete to put back over the blocks.

Now, I had to tackle the smell in the property. I noticed that all the walls were a slightly brown colour. I sprayed the very top of the wall in the lounge and immediately noticed that this strong degreaser I was using was starting to make the evaporated body fat that was stuck to the walls run. I proceeded to wash down all the walls in the property, removing what must have been litres of evaporated body matter that had been missed by the previous companies.

Lo and behold, by the time I'd finished, the odour had gone. This set a great precedent for us working with insurance companies and loss adjusters in the future. I travelled back to West Wales, having earned over £5000 on that job, and for one of the first times, felt like I was a specialist in my field—a professional—having managed to work out what had happened and being able to fix it when others had failed.

A call came in to attend a property where someone had died; apparently, the smell was horrendous! You never quite know what to make of comments like these, as very often people exaggerate… but oh my goodness, they were not wrong!

I remember opening the door without my mask on and whoof, I was hit by the smell of decomposed matter! It was a small flat where a young man lived who had died and not been found. This can be common in cities and large towns, but in sleepy West Wales, where everyone knows everyone, it's strange for no one to realise a young man had passed away…

For this reason, the police installed spy cameras into the property to see if anyone else had attended after the death, I presume in an effort to rule out any possible foul play, such as poisoning, or so someone could return to steal anything from the property.

Either way, we had the task of lifting all the carpet tiles first… Carpet tiles have a rubber backing that makes saturation into the flooring a little different from most carpets – instead of just soaking through, the fluid follows gaps and cambers in the flooring – meaning that you can easily get fluid travel metres from the actual area the person was found at.

Lifting the tiles, we noticed a chipboard floor underneath that was also saturated and had bulged and expanded from the amount of moisture it had been exposed to. The sofa the man had died on was saturated in black decomposed body fat, with a sleeping bag pushed up that was full of maggots and larvae cases.

There was an undeniable mark on the front of the sofa where the undertaker had slid the body off and into polythene and then into a body bag to remove – (body bags are normally so strong that they cope with most things – although we have had to clean a few stairwells where the bag has burst when the undertaker was carrying it down… not pleasant to clean!!).

After slicing through the flooring with a circular saw, we lifted the soaked floorboards… what we saw underneath took us back! Normally under flooring, you expect to see a small void about 6-10 inches deep – with services like electrics, pipework, etc., running through it… Under this floor was a void about 4 feet deep!! And what looked like a suspended ceiling below that, all covered in maggots and body fluid.

We couldn't work it out for a moment, as the flat was at ground level and the door to it opened onto a road. We then realised that there was another building below that was accessed from another road behind the building that was lower – and, in fact, it was a women's clothes shop underneath.

I walked around the property, down onto the lower street, and went into the shop. I asked for the manager and asked her if she had any bad smells in the shop.

She said, "Yes! We think we have a dead rat above the changing room!"

I explained it wasn't a dead rat, but rather a decomposed body, and the maggots she had found on the changing room floor were not from a rodent but a human body that was above! You can imagine her reaction!

As she led us to the changing room, we looked up at the suspended ceiling to a brown stain.

She said, "Is that him?"

I said, "It's some of him!!"

Maybe now is a good time to briefly discuss PPE (personal protective equipment). To be honest, the methods we have put in place are our first line of defence, the products we use are our second defence, and finally, PPE is our safety net. What it does is offer a barrier between us and the horrendous situations we clean up.

Gloves mean we lose the sense of touch. Safety goggles or visors sit between our skin and eyes, and our amazing masks remove the sense of smell, which is really appreciated.

When I see the clean-up teams on the news looking for bodies after disasters in hot countries with just paper masks on, my heart goes out to them!

Shotgun Suicide

More common than you think, and I bet it's a scene you've never even imagined having to be cleaned by someone…

So, who owns a shotgun? Well, most farmers, but many of the public also own shotguns. Some shoot for fun, and you can even own a shotgun licence at 16 years old if you are a member of a gun club! Bizarre, you're not allowed to drink or smoke at 16 years old… but you can own a shotgun!

The sad reality is that when used for suicide, the fallout is awful. I have cleaned up loads of trauma scenes following the deployment of a shotgun. If you've ever seen a shotgun cartridge, you will notice that if you shake it, it rattles. This is because it's full of tiny balls of lead or steel shot. The spray from the barrel is violent, powerful, and pretty sporadic. Some cleans have been on beds and armchairs, some in yards, sheds, piggeries, or farmyards. The hardest to clean are often on staircases in houses.

One of the worst shotgun suicide scenes I encountered was at a remote farm in West Wales. The man had taken his life on the first few steps of the stairwell. As I entered the front door, the stairs were straight in front of me. Normally, the undertaker takes most parts of the body, but on this occasion, large pieces of the skull and pieces of brain were on the stairs. The sides of the stairwell were wallpapered with woodchip wallpaper, and all the way up the stairs were holes from the shot, tufts of hair, pieces of flesh, bone, and blood spatter. There is also a really sticky, shiny fluid, which I think is cerebrospinal fluid from around the brain, that is always present on shotgun suicides.

Looking at this sight would be enough to give most people nightmares, but I tend to see pound signs! I try to think of what the place will look like after I have finished when I hand the property back to the family or solicitors. A long task is ahead, working inwards and upwards to sanitise, clean, repair, and decorate the area, and remove all the waste.

Another memorable clean-up involving a shotgun suicide was of a young lad who was only 16. As mentioned, you can legally own a shotgun at 16 years old in the UK if you're a member of a shooting club at the time of writing this book. The scene was so sad, and worst still was the story behind it… This young lad had split up with his girlfriend, had a couple of drinks, and took his own life in his bedroom while his family were downstairs! Imagine having to go through that as parents! My heart goes out to anyone in this situation.

As with any shotgun, the fallout was large and all over the room. Sanitising, scraping, and wiping each surface took hours to remove every residue from the room. Finding even whole earlobes with an earring stud still intact, removing it, cleaning it, and placing the earring in a box for the family. The waste comprised of blood-soaked bedding, a mattress soaked through with blood and synovial fluid. The bed turned out to be a sofa bed, and the body fluid had soaked through into the bed base where the bed tucks away to reveal a sofa. The only odour from this type of death clean-up is sometimes the lingering smell of gunpowder from the deployment, followed by a strong iron smell – typically what you smell in butchers or abattoirs. We cleaned the property meticulously and handed the keys back to the police, who were dealing with the family.

Some scenes can become really complicated. Another shotgun suicide was in Pembrokeshire, where a gentleman deployed a shotgun in a conservatory on the side of his house! Not only were there fragments of skull and matter embedded into the polycarbonate roof, but the exterior wall of the house was also pebble-dashed with tiny multi-coloured stones! This meant we had to decipher what was red stone and what was body matter. The roof had to be removed and deemed as potentially infectious waste, and the clean took a few days to remove and replace everything that was affected – including a new roof! I remember going through items in the room and cleaning them as we went –the ferocity of the fallout was such that pieces of skull were even found inside shoes and in coat pockets!

Myself and my team have, and continue, to clean up sadly hundreds of suicides each year. They are sad places to be during the clean. You are in a position to see where a person spent their last thoughts and moments – and for whatever reason, they decided to take their life. I still cannot relate to how they must feel and what's going through their minds.

I did read an amazing book called Reasons to Stay Alive by Matt Haig in order to relate somehow to those who suffer from depression and are in dire straits. It's an amazing book and worth a read.

Some suicides we clean-up are very violent, and you can tell they were spur-of-the- moment decisions. Some are calculated, with every little point considered. My own great uncle took his life. He was Italian and lived in Tuscany, and he cared for his wife, who suffered from dementia and had been in a home for many years. He would, I am told, visit her daily, and as soon as she passed away, he rang my Nonno (his brother) to tell him he was about to take his own life. He had sorted all his affairs and even booked himself into a crematorium! No matter how fast my mum and my Nonno got to Italy, they were too late.

We attended one scene where a man emptied his house completely, cleaned every surface, made a makeshift paddling pool with a kids' wigwam over it, and even placed mirrors inside to watch himself as he bled out. He too had booked his own cremation and notified the police to call and find him! Leaving us just the simple clean-up of the paddling pool and the 8/10 pints of blood he left after the coroner had removed him.

Another scene I worked on that was difficult was at a

biomass plant. These are vast buildings with a constant feed of timber on one side, which is burned to power huge generators that push electricity back into the grid. The buildings are large industrial buildings the size of football pitches and some as high as 100ft, with gantries, viewing platforms, and an array of moving hot machinery.

One worker at the plant we were called to decontaminate had decided to take his life by putting a ratchet strap around his neck and jumping from a 40ft gantry. He was instantly decapitated, with his head being catapulted up onto a ledge about 40 feet above, whilst his body fell 40ft onto a rotating machine. The fallout over such a large distance, coupled with the temperature and moving machinery, made it a really difficult clean. The only upside for us was that the floor was covered with sawdust, making the floor easier to clean.

As we arrived, the SOCO met us and said: "This is an interesting one. There's some of him here," pointing to the ledge, "some of him here...," pointing to the wall, "and a lot of him here," pointing to the floor.

I remember what a sombre place it was to clean, with all the staff – his colleagues knowing what had happened and possibly seeing it – all sitting in the staff room drinking coffee and chatting. I had to take ladders to get to the ledge on the wall where his head finally rested, and clean up all the fluid that was left behind.

Next was to try and clean a machine that his body had fallen onto, which was still being used and could not be switched off. I had to scrape and wipe blood and tissue out of machine parts that were hot and moving in places!

It was a challenging job, both emotionally and physically. And one where, again, we were on the scene very quickly following the death. But we were super proud that we managed to clean it all down and remove a scene that would have caused others severe trauma.

What I call …. Cat Women

There have been so many of these jobs I have done – I have lost count, not exactly a crime scene – but certainly worth a mention!

Imagine the scene – environmental health has called a few times to the property and explained that the property needs to be cleaned up, the smell is affecting neighbours, and rats have been seen running up the curtains by passers-by! The environmental health team does all they can to encourage the person to clean up – but when it all fails, they ask us to go in and clean. This is paid for by the council serving an order on the property, which means that when the property is ever sold in the future, the local authority gets their money back for the work needed.

We meet the environmental health officer at the property, and we are led through the hallway where there are four cats sitting on furniture, and who are using anything they choose to urinate and defecate on. The smell of ammonia and filth, coupled with the immense temperature of the house (the heating was blasting in mid-summer), fills the air. We are led through to the kitchen, where the officer says:

"Margret – these are the cleaners I told you about."

Margret is sitting on what can only be described as a throne of empty crisp packets and empty 1-litre lemonade bottles. There must have been thousands of empty packets around her, and each time she moved, something would fall off the throne and either drift to the floor like a leaf in autumn or bounce away down the kitchen. A pyramid about 18 inches high of used tea bags sat on the drainer of the sink. About 8-10 cats were perched on furniture, her lap, or on some old scratching posts dotted around!

Margret was in a sorry state, wearing some old cotton tracksuit bottoms and a filthy knitted jumper. Apparently, she couldn't walk, hardly spoke, and smelled like everything else in the house! The officer looked at me and said:

"This is a good room! Margret – I am just going to show them the house."

Margret nodded, and we headed into the lounge. The door was only open enough to squeeze through. I tried to push the door, but it wouldn't open any further. It wasn't until I squeezed inside the lounge that I realised I had stepped up at least 18 inches into what can only be described as the biggest litter tray I had ever seen! The whole room was at least 18 inches deep in cat faeces – the smell was horrendous, and the ammonia made my eyes start to water! At least four cats were in the middle of defecating while we were in there! Every room had at least two cats in it, and one had over 10 kittens playing on a bed, crawling and falling off the sides!

I thought this would be perfect for filming and asked the officer to ask Margret if we could film the clean-up. She left us and then came back, saying Margret was happy for us to film. Amazing! I called the film crew and said we would return tomorrow to make a start.

You have no idea what was to happen the following morning!

Myself and two staff arrived and parked up. Then, the film crew arrived, and we prepared them for the scene, explaining Margret's situation and her sad demeanour. We all put on white suits and A1P2 masks to stop us from smelling the foul odour. The RSPCA were next to arrive, as Margret had agreed for all but three of the cats to be taken away to be re-homed. We all stood in line, ready to enter the house of filth!

I knocked at the door – opening the key safe, removing the key. I was just about to unlock the door when it swung open.

"HELLO, everyone, lovely to see you all!" Margret (who we all thought was unable to walk) greeted us like a film star. She was dressed in her wedding dress from forty years ago, her face covered in white powder and bright red lipstick, which was more on her face than on her lips.

I turned round to the cameraman, who looked around from the eyepiece of his video camera and mouthed, "What the hell?"

Margret then proceeded to offer us all crisps and lemonade, which she had set out on a table literally covered in cat faeces, cat hair, and dirt. We all politely declined, apart from the RSPCA guy, who helped himself to two packets of cheese and onion crisps!

We started in the lounge/litter tray, and with every shovel full we removed, we uncovered years of cat faeces, intertwined with worms, beetles, and the odd item of household cutlery and crockery that was buried in it. Finally, at the base, there was a well-rotted carpet! We removed over four tonnes of waste from the lounge alone!

After a few days of hard graft, we left Margret sitting on a clean armchair we collected from a charity, with a new mattress and bedding to allow her and her three cats to sleep on, and the house smelling fresh and clean.

Wow, she was a character!

Geraldine was another one I remember! This time, as we entered her house with another environmental officer, we were greeted with expletives and shouting and told to clear off! This wasn't going to happen, as there was a warrant to allow for cleaning to take place. Geraldine screamed at the officer, threw a teacup at him, and ran out the back door, down the garden, and into an old touring caravan she slept in.

"Good," said the officer. "Now she's gone, we can begin!" "Throw anything covered in cat sh@t in the skip!" Easier said than done, as almost everything in every room was covered in cat faeces! The officer left, and Geraldine returned, begging us not to throw away a copy of a Woman's Weekly magazine from 1975 that was dripping in poo, as there was a recipe she wanted in it!

I took the opportunity to ask her why the cat litter trays – of which there were many, all full of pristine clean new litter – were not being used by the cats. The reply still makes me laugh and cringe. Geraldine replied, "Oh, the cats stopped using them when my husband started using them!"

Enough said.

As I looked down at her feet, I noticed she was wearing red jelly sandals, and the gaps in her toes were all full of cat poo. I realised I was not going to make any difference to her way of thinking!

We filled the skip full to bursting, and I called the skip company and asked for a replacement for 7am the next day. We left, feeling that although Geraldine didn't appreciate it, we were making her life better bit by bit.

That all changed the next morning. We arrived on-site at 6:45am to make a good start and hopefully finish, greeted by an empty skip ready to fill. I was so impressed by the skip company… until we opened the door to the house and realised that not only had Geraldine emptied the skip herself, but she had put everything, and I mean everything, back where it came from! She had been up all night undoing all we had done! And at 7am on the dot, another skip arrived, the driver looking puzzled at what he was supposed to swap it with.

Unfortunately for Geraldine, she had worked so hard that she was exhausted and asleep in the caravan. So we all put in a massive shift and filled the skip again while the driver waited. Then we filled the second skip that afternoon and stayed on-site until that was removed as well by the skip company.

Geraldine awoke, screaming at us and throwing stuff at us, but our job was done, and we left the environmental officer there with her to smooth things out!

Little did she know, the RSPCA were on their way to take away 30 of her feline friends! Glad I wasn't there for that.

Daughter lived in house with deceased mum for years

We have dealt with some strange situations and even stranger people over the years. One job, which we were asked to carry out an environmental cleaning on, was of interest to not only environmental health but also the police. It was a property where a 45-year-old lady lived. She was a hoarder, and when you entered the house, the hallway was pretty clear, but each room was full from floor to ceiling with collected items and rubbish. We had the heads-up from the police that we may possibly come across human remains during the clean, and if so, we were to contact them immediately. They supplied an officer at the front door when we arrived.

The lady who lived there was remarkably calm and collected, and you would never have known she lived in such a state if you had bumped into her while shopping or walking. Sure enough, we started working our way into the property, and about three to four tonnes into the clearance, our team came across bones. We were not sure if they were animal or human. The clean stopped, and the officer at the door was notified. Three days later, we were informed that we could proceed and that the remains were, in fact, the lady's mother, who had died in the property! She had just covered her body with rubbish and carried on with her life. It was estimated that the body had been there for some twenty years. The smell would have stopped a few months after she had passed away, but the reality of the fact that she was still there must have been weird. How someone could do that is beyond me… living in a house, knowing that your mother's corpse was in the room, covered with rubbish for years!

The whale!

Now and again, we get a strange job… I mean strange to us! I appreciate that many of these jobs are strange to most normal people! Again, picture the scene… My parents have a holiday complex; it's closed for the New Year for maintenance, and after helping my dad grout the swimming pool, I now find myself in a pool full of cold water that's heating up. On New Year's Day, I'm changing an underwater light!

This involves me in a pool with some diving weights I borrowed from a mate, a wetsuit, and a hosepipe connected to a snorkel to allow me to breathe while underwater, connecting the new light up!

I get a call from my colleague, Mark… I come up to take the call as I can hear the phone ringing.

Mark says, "Have you seen the email?"

"No," I said.

"You need to see the email," he says!

So, my dad passes me a towel to dry my hands, and I begin to scroll through my emails while standing in a pool in a wetsuit with a snorkel on! Dad says, "Can't they leave you alone for five minutes?" and "Just leave it, go on…"

I scroll through and see a picture of a whale hanging over the bow of a large ship!

With the message, "Can you or do you deal with dead whales?" Mark calls back and says, “Shall I reply, ‘No’?”

I said, “NOOOOO, we can do it – I know a guy!”

Locally to us is a man and his wife who are truly an amazing couple. Not only do they know all there is to know about wildlife, but he works for a company that collects and monitors stranded marine life.

I finish the pool light with Dad and drive over to his house, armed with one picture of this whale over a ship's bow!

He says, "Come in, want a coffee?" and when I show him the picture, he says, "It's a fin whale, probably 20m long. It was probably hit whilst sleeping on the surface," which I later found to be exactly true! Wow, he knew his stuff!! He said his colleague in England would help if they could have samples for studying – of course, I said yes, and I was so grateful for his help. We are bizarrely neighbours now. His colleague gave me the name of a rendering plant where we could take it… so now, after calling them, all I have to do is arrange transport from Portsmouth, where the ship is to dock, to the rendering plant! Thank goodness for what happened next!

I was trying to call friends who had large waste lorries, walking trailers for unloading bulk waste, and even a large flatbed when someone told me of a video on YouTube where a Taiwanese guy transporting a dead whale decided to drive through a town to show the locals the dead whale he was moving on a flatbed, strapped down. But right in the middle of the town, it exploded due to the gases inside it and the tension from the straps! It covered the town and people in rotting whale blubber and intestines!

This made me rethink the travel plans, and I called the rendering plant and asked who they use. They said, "We have our own lorries!" He asked the size, and I had been told 10m long by the port… when it was lifted out, it was, in fact, 22m long!!

So, the rendering team arrived armed with massive butchery knives to cut it in half to put onto their tub lorries. Our team on-site then realised that the mouth was too large for the trailer and had to nip off and buy a motorised saw to cut the mouth off to fit it in…

They then set about cleaning up the fallout from the dissection!

A great effort with great results – with thanks to our team in Portsmouth, Jim, and Total Trauma Cleaning for helping us out.

We made a small fortune from saying yes to that job… and it was all to do with the relationships I have made over the years. You may wonder how I was able to call on Jim to help… This is due to our amazing training academy, which I will tell you about later.

One cool thing I found out was that whale oil is used to lubricate satellites in space – as it is one, if not the only, oil that doesn't freeze!

April Jones

We have attended some high-profile cleans, many of which I am not at liberty to discuss. The sad account of April Jones being killed by Mark Bridger was a house I attended. Sadly, the remains of April have never been found. When I was taken to the property by the police, it was bizarrely just to clean up mouse droppings!

The reason is that when the jury attends the property of a serious incident, the scene has to replicate the scent that the officers originally found when they first attended the scene. There had to be food in the cupboards, and there were no mouse droppings on the floor or surfaces! So, all I was asked to do was to return to the property before the jury attended each visit and vacuum all the surfaces.

This case was a tragic one, and entering the property felt strange as I had learned so much of the events from officers and the press. The house has since been demolished. Again, my heart goes out to the family, friends, and officers who were involved in this horrendous event.

Drip Drip

Please help, we have a brown liquid dripping off our lightbulb in the lounge – it seems to be coming from above. The smell is terrible. The flat was in Wimbledon. I drove from West Wales, and when I got there, four hours later, I could tell instantly the smell was of a dead body! They had a baby who was in a walker on the floor. There was a consistent drip onto the floor, and the lightbulb was heating up the fluid, making the smell much worse!

I asked about the flat above – an elderly gentleman lived there, apparently. I said, "Have you seen him lately?" The look on her face suddenly changed.

"Do you think it's him?" she said, staring and starting to shake. "I think so!" She screamed at her partner and said, "We're leaving now!" Grabbing the child, they ran outside.

"Whatever it costs, we will pay – call us when it's sorted!"

I went upstairs and knocked on the door. No answer. I opened the letterbox, and instantly, the smell hit me! So I called the police and waited for them to come. They brought a locksmith to break in and confirmed there was a body inside.

I booked into a hotel for the night and waited for the police to let me know if I could gain access. That night, the police confirmed the body had been removed, and they had given my number to the family connected to the gentleman. Sure enough, I had a call from a family in France who were related and asked me to clean the flat.

The next day, I cleaned the top flat, removed the soiled carpet and flooring, cleaned and sealed the void below, deodorised the whole flat, and then cleaned and sealed the ceiling in the flat below and repainted it. I changed the light pendant and called the family to tell them it was all clear.

One of my best paydays – two properties sorted in one day! The family from France also asked us the week after to empty the flat for them to market with an estate agent. So we did really, really well out of that job!

Drugs .. what Drugs?

A distraught ex-wife calls us to say that she has a property in Scotland that needs cleaning and clearing following the death of her ex-husband. We asked for details and were told that he was a lovely guy, sadly passed away naturally, and the police had the keys to the property.

"Please can we clean, sanitise, and empty the flat so that it can be handed back to the local authority for new tenants?"

Our team was dispatched and called us on arrival. They had found some bags of powder in a cupboard. We called the police and asked if they had checked the property, which they said they had, and there was nothing found of any concern.

We asked them to reattend to check what the team had found, only to discover that it was class A drugs with a street value of £200k! Not sure how that got missed!

When we told his ex-wife, she was completely puzzled and had no idea that he had any connection to drugs.

We never found out why or what on this one—just thought it was a memorable clean! And proof that you never know what people are doing or what you will find!

Hoarders

These are a group of amazing people who always make me feel a raft of emotions for them. If you've seen the TV series *Buried Alive*, genuinely, you haven't seen anything! I have cleaned up so, so many properties where the owners cannot throw anything away – and I mean anything! We've emptied chest freezers of human poo, each turd wrapped in newspaper and stacked onto a freezer. One house I emptied had over 2,000 bottles of urine – and these were 2-litre bottles – where the owner, a man, was peeing into a Frugi milkshake bottle and then decanting into larger soft drink bottles to store!

I have found lines of bottle tops sellotaped together to make 3-metre-long strings, and in one house, there were over 40 of these strings! One quite disturbing find was what we thought were a selection of wax balls – only to realise they were, in fact, nose bogey balls! Each the size of cricket balls, made from thousands of nose pickings!

These houses are also served warrants by the council for environmental and fire risk reasons. One of these was lived in by a little man in a wheelchair. We were greeted by the usual expletives telling us to go forth and multiply! But this guy started to swing his walking stick at me as I started bagging up what was rubbish to you and me, but treasure to him! It got to the point where he put his cigarette out on my back, and we had to call the police and get him arrested. He left in the back of a police van.

He was a circular hoarder! He loved anything round – coins glued together in strips, bottle tops, drinks cans, etc. We were happily throwing them all into waste sacks when we came across a load of Marvel milk containers – round, foil-lined tubes with an aluminium base and a plastic lid – like giant Pringles tubes. We'd thrown about 50 of them already, and these had gone to the waste transfer station before one of the lads threw one at me as a joke. I ducked, and it hit the floor, popping the top off and revealing a wad of cash inside. We opened what we had left, and it amounted to £17,000!

We went to the recycling centre, but they said they had found nothing… We didn't believe them! So, when the guy returned from custody, we left the environmental health officer to hand the money back to him. We have always been 100% honest, and I think, with all the cash and valuables we've handed over to family and authorities, it's given us a good name locally and been a reason for us picking up so much of this type of work.

You may want to have a trawl through the videos on TikTok or YouTube and search for a clean-up of a World War 2 bunker in Pembrokeshire. We had a film crew follow us on this one for a series on ITV. A lady was living in an underground World War 2 bunker, with no lights apart from a candle, water running in from the walls and ceilings, and she had accumulated over 4 tonnes of rubbish she was living on. Along with – I kid you not… her pet horse! The RSPCA removed the horse before we started. When we arrived at the bunker, we had to attach a festoon of portable lights to the ceiling, and it wasn't until we removed all the rubbish that we realised the floors were over 3 feet deep in rubbish. This meant that, when we removed it all, we couldn't reach our lights to take any with us!

Uncovering litter, waste mixed with rodent carcasses, and then finding an exercise trampoline buried in one corner. The lady watched us the whole time, and then, when we were nearly finished, she disclosed the bombshell that she was a cleaning supervisor for another local cleaning company! It gave me a massive sense of pride completing this job. When we arrived, the lady was living in an awful state, and after removing all the filth, rodents, and waste, we went to a local charity and got her a clean bed and bedding. We walked away, feeling we had given her a second chance! It's probably in the same state again, with another horse in tow … but at the time, it felt good!

Gender?

This word throws up all sorts of conversations these days... but I feel I should mention that when I first started this work, it was a very male-oriented business. However, I am proud to say that I have trained hundreds of women who have joined the ranks of our network and are now outstanding biohazard cleaners. It's been such a pleasure to work with them and help their businesses grow and flourish.

The Arm

Rarely do we encounter whole limbs to collect or remove – normally, the coroner office or the undertaker removes these. It's actually law in the UK that a body must be buried or cremated with all body parts that are available. But sometimes, we find bits and bobs that we have to ask the undertaker to return!

Some jobs just get bizarre and are complicated. We were called to an office in London where an oil company operated from, a stunning office looking over the Thames. All we were told was that we needed a team that not only could deal with biohazards but also needed rope access and confined space training.

When our team arrived, we were told what happened – a lift engineer had been called to repair or service the lift. Thinking he had isolated the lift, he opened the door and reached inside the lift shaft to check something. When the lift was called from another floor, the mechanism trapped his arm and, unfortunately, severed it! He was taken to A&E for treatment. Someone apparently tried to lower the lift and catch his arm as it fell, but sadly missed it, and it fell to the bottom of the lift shaft.

We were asked to attend, recover the arm, and decontaminate the lift shaft. Sadly, it took two days before we were allowed to enter the lift shaft after the HSE had investigated! By that time, not only had the arm started to decompose, but there were also rats in the lift shaft that had been busy! There was also a really expensive wristwatch on the arm that needed to be handed to the family!

We recovered what was left and cleaned and sanitised the lift shaft. The combination of a biohazard-trained, confined space-trained, and rope access-trained team made this job incredibly lucrative – again, we solved a really, really difficult problem with our amazing teams.

Connections

The larger our network became, the more connections were seen between jobs that came in and out of teams. Let me explain – when I was travelling from West Wales all over the UK decontaminating properties, I had zero connections to what I was cleaning, but now we have teams in most areas. They sometimes have direct connections to the tragedy.

One of these was a call that came in from North Wales. A gentleman had gotten out of his car to right a signpost that had blown down on the road. As he opened his door, a large lorry hit him, dragging him down the road. His remains were along the road and also caught up in the wheel arch, bumper, cab, and side of the lorry. We were asked to attend a truck stop where the lorry had been parked around the back – to clean and decontaminate it.

We have an amazing team in Manchester with a good friend, Wayne, who owns Bespoke Cleaning – a really professional outfit who we work with most weeks. Wayne said he could sort the job, and we passed over all the details. It was only after the job that Wayne heard the local news while on his way to his second home in North Wales. He called me and said,

"You know that guy that was hit by the lorry... he was my handyman for the house in Wales! I've been trying to get hold of him."

This kind of thing is happening more and more as the

network grows and we use local teams to sort local work.

You may recall an event in Plymouth, UK, on August 12th, 2021. A man called Jake Davison walked through the streets of Keyham with a shotgun and killed five people, including his mother, injured two others, and then took his own life. You can imagine the trauma this caused in Keyham.

We had a team just a stone's throw away, run by two amazing people, Ken and Leanne,

and they accepted the job. (Ken sadly passed away himself recently after a long fight with cancer. He was a great colleague, a truly professional and hardworking man with an amazing sense of humour. He will be truly missed by all who knew him.)

Facts were not immediately disclosed by the police in regard to those he had killed, and it was only when on site that Ken and Leanne realised they knew some of the victims and their family personally. Although it was incredibly traumatic cleaning up the remains on the pathways of these innocent victims, Leanne told me she felt incredibly honoured to be able to do something positive for the community at that time. Our hearts go out to all those who were affected.

Again, I can't reiterate how amazing our network is.

Faith

Since being a teenager, I have always had a strong faith in a creator. I grew up by a small beach called Mwnt and would spend most of my summers there or on the farm, watching animals being born, dolphins in the bay, amazing sunsets, and seeing this incredible world firsthand.

I have tried desperately to prove to myself, with help from my science and biology teachers, that life could just exist without anything, or that there can't be a designer behind the design I see in the most simple lifeforms. Believe me, not feeling accountable or part of a purpose is far simpler and far easier to live by! But each day I am more and more convinced of a designer. I don't really like religion—I see it as such a reason for negativity in the world—but I also see no correlation between a creator and most religions.

I decided to make an in-depth study of the Bible to see if it held the answers to the questions I had. Mum had been a Buddhist, Dad was Church of England but never went. They both began studying the Bible together with friends, and this thirst for wanting to know more encouraged me to study as well.

So, at the time of writing this, myself and my family all have a strong faith in the God of the Bible, Jehovah. It's helped me with so many burning questions, like what's the purpose for the planet and mankind, why is there so much suffering, and will things change in the future?

What was really strange was that, inadvertently, I realised I had built a business that, according to the Bible, was pretty future-proof for the time being! See if you agree at 2 Timothy 3:1–4.

I really think that my faith, and my amazing wife and kids, have been the stabilising foundation that's got me through lots of what I have seen and experienced, and they have always been the grounding that I have needed to stay as humble and kind as I can. I make mistakes on a daily basis, like anyone, and each day is a learning curve, but I genuinely feel it's been the best thing I have ever done for myself and my family.

Training

When I first started this business, I realised that it was all reactive. That meant it would be really difficult to have teams of people all over the country waiting for work to come in as part of their day-to-day work. I needed to create a reactive team that would either drop work they were doing and react to specialist work, or would be available at the drop of a hat, day or night, to carry out biohazard reactive cleaning.

I also realised that this business had to be one that offered national coverage and national rates, as many of our clients were also nationwide and bound by budgets. But I also realised that for a company to employ staff to cover things like road traffic accidents and decontamination work out of hours, they would have to employ at least four to five staff to cover the shift patterns required, holiday and sickness cover, and also have a vehicle equipped and ready to react.

Therefore, if we could create a network of trained subcontractors, we could compete for this work commercially and professionally.

I had a mate, Mark Baxter, who I'd been friends with for a while. He had worked in the vehicle industry, but most importantly, had managed quite a large team. I asked him if he would help me build a network of specialist cleaning teams, and to my amazement, he said he was in!

Mark and I set about marketing, building a training

course, and testing the water to see if we could find anyone as crazy as us to be a part of it.

I wrote the training manual, which I felt needed at least three days of training to deliver. I managed to partner with some specialist pest control companies, specialist chemical providers, and asked a couple of friends who were also power tool trainers and health and safety trainers to join us in delivering the training.

The training, which was initially called the National Academy of Crime Scene Cleaners, has now effectively been used to train over 3,000 people in the UK and Europe, and has since been rebranded as the Ultima Cleaning Academy. We've had some real memorable experiences with trainees fainting, crying when seeing some of the scenes that we have cleaned, and arriving for training without telling us they have one arm or a leg missing (which has created its own problems – all of which we've overcome).

The training covers pest control at a crime scene, including flies and maggots, hypodermic needle collection, waste disposal and legislation, methodology on cleaning crime scenes and biohazard clean-up, saturated floor removal, health and safety training and legislation, marketing and pricing, along with practical sessions including body fluid removal from carpeting, flooring, and furniture, hypodermic needle removal from inside and outside spaces, road traffic accident clean-up, and the correct use of fogging machines for decontamination.

At first, the training was just face-to-face, but now it's available as e-learning, which has been better for many who can't afford the time to travel to our training centre. If you get a chance have a look at www.ultimaenvironmental.com or www.ultimacleaningacademy.com if it's something you are interested in doing for yourself.

It's strange how our training is now recognised throughout the UK, and demanded by many public and private sector businesses. And to think it all started with a thought in my head in West Wales. I recently saw a tender for cleaning body fluid off train carriages in Northern Ireland, which stated that to qualify, you must have completed training with Ultima Cleaning Academy or similar. This gave me an amazing sense of pride.

We chose to carry out our training in Bristol as it was central to the UK and had good rail, road, and airport access. We used to rent a building off Bristol Zoo to carry out the training. You can imagine how difficult it was to approach a hotel and ask if we could, in one room, train staff using PowerPoint, and in the next room, have a number of scenarios set up, such as bedrooms, lounges, and kitchens, and cover the furniture with needles, fake blood, and chicken skin for practical training. Needless to say, renting an old stable block was the way forward! As the buildings adjacent to ours were still used by Bristol Zoo, it also came with its challenges.

Like the time I was training a team on floor removal in the courtyard, while Wayne, our H&S officer, was training the other half of the group in the training room down the road. We were supposed to both finish in about an hour and swap the groups over, until, while we were in mid-floor cutting, a Spanish lady from the zoo's reception shouted, "GET INSIDE! GET INSIDE!! WE HAVE A SITUATION!!" Panic ensued, and we all ran into the main building, to be told that a lynx had escaped!

We were all huddled in this room, looking out the windows trying to spot the cat. It was funny for about 20 minutes. Then Wayne phoned, "Where are you guys?" My reply wasn't what he was expecting. "Trapped in a room as a lynx is on the loose!" An hour went by with no news. I went to reception and said, "We need to go." This little lady, Said, with her strong Andalusian accent, said, "You can't... the lynx!" I said, "We can run to our cars and head straight out." She said, "Who will open the gate?" I said, "I will." "Oh, you're so brave," came the reply! More stupid, I feel!! But needs must.

I don't think they ever retrieved the lynx, and it was only at this time that I decided to google how many animals Bristol Zoo had lost over the years. It's frightening! So, probably due to the possibility of this happening again and a needed change in venue, we brought an Arctic wagon with an exhibition unit on the back, and we now use this for all our practical training needs.

At the time of writing this book, we now have over 300 teams nationwide, who can react within two hours to any decontamination required. They're all trained, managed, insured, inoculated, and equipped, and are truly an amazing team. I have so much admiration for them, and for the loyalty and trust they've shown in us as an Academy. Not only have we trained them, but we've also found them work and helped them progress in this specialist industry.

We are now working with our Scottish counterpart, Jamie Hughes, who initially trained with us to be a trauma cleaner, but who now helps manage and train our new network cohorts. In the early days of the formation of our training Academy, it was mainly a male-oriented business. But it is so lovely to see now that we have amazing teams of male and female specialist cleaners who are tackling some of the most horrendous scenes on a day-to-day basis.

COVID

When COVID hit, we were in a prime position to offer decontamination services nationally. With teams in almost every part of the UK and Southern Ireland, we were the go-to supplier for national banks, stores, airlines, and many other companies who wanted a quick solution backed up by a professional company that could respond anywhere within two hours.

If I am honest, we never saw an increase in cleaning up after death. We were just used to sanitising and decontaminating buildings, offices, and aircraft. We were working with the likes of Ryanair, EasyJet, Barclays, JD Sports, HMCTS courts, to name just a few. It became relentless and got to a point where my team were not even sleeping some nights as they were managing thirty-forty jobs that were coming in daily.

But we weathered the storm. Our network worked tirelessly, each member earning thousands, and we also did amazingly well. Finally, the network was used for what we had proposed: national call-outs, national rates, and a totally managed and supported network.

Again, it's hard to think that this all started in my head twenty years earlier.

Some memorable jobs during COVID included flying a team out to Athens to decontaminate an aeroplane for Ryanair before port health would allow it to take off, helping EasyJet to make their "We're Flying Again" video and design a method for them to sanitise their aircraft, being ferried out to clean two massive shipping tankers where all the crew had gone down with COVID, cleaning a submarine, helicopters off the Scottish coast, vast trading floors in Canary Wharf, film studios and actors' Winnebagos, even Tom Cruise's Mission: Impossible film set, loads of distilleries, and even a few Premier League football grounds.

Wow, it was a busy time, and it seemed for the first time nationally that all the hard work had paid off. All the knowledge I had acquired about bacteria and viruses, the relationships we had made with chemists and distributors, the training programme, and the relationship with our network—all became worth it!

Ollie

You never know what life will throw at you, and a few years ago, my son, at the age of 16, was diagnosed with stage 4 lymphoma cancer – the fittest and, we thought, the healthiest member of our family. Wow, that was a tough time for all our family to go through, and like so many others, we found ourselves on the rollercoaster that is cancer treatment. I only mention this as running a business is difficult when all is great, let alone when your child is poorly.

Everyone in the business was amazing, friends and family were rocks, and the local community were so supportive. All those years we had donated to local charities, supported foundations and events, and helped to raise money for those in need made sense when we were on the receiving end! A massive thanks to the TCT in Cardiff, Maggie's in Swansea, and Dr. Boulter, our GP, who was so amazing.

Ollie survived after chemotherapy and radiotherapy, and now lives in Newcastle where he is happily married and healthy, having had the all-clear a couple of years ago. I am super proud of him and Maddie, my daughter. Ollie works a 40-hour shift and is building his own gym clothing brand called GymRats on the side, while Maddie is self-employed as a dog groomer and also has a thriving pottery business - both are hard working and what I love most - entrepreneurial!

What Now

As you can imagine, the business grew and became an animal in its own right. Still serving as its MD, I now work part-time, and the business is owned by a large FM company that acquired it two years ago. I still love being involved, training people, and seeing it grow. The amazing network we created is out there every day of the year, cleaning up following tragic and violent deaths, and I am thankful to all of them for their hard work and friendship. To all the families that have been torn apart through tragedy – I am so, so sorry for your losses. My heart goes out to you all.

My wife and I, along with our daughter, also run a small farm with Highland cattle, nestled in the countryside of West Wales. Yes, I still live where I love living, with the people I love. Business-wise, I have a few other business interests and am busy every day doing what I love. Constantly looking for new opportunities, I still find myself bored at the slightest quiet point… Let's see what the future brings!

Dedication

I would like to dedicate this to Mum and Dad – the entrepreneur hippies, my amazing wife Linz, my children Maddie and Ollie and all my friends and family who I love,

Acknowledgements

I would like to thank all the team at Ultima, Mark Baxter, Jamie Hughes, Pete Swanick, Jamie B, Nicola, Helen, Elise, Johnny and his team of grafters, and all the network of amazing people we have trained and work with on a daily basis.

Printed in Dunstable, United Kingdom

71407247R00077